D1709133

MYSTERIES, LEGENDS, AND UNEXPLAINED PHENOMENA

MAGIC AND ALCHEMY

MYSTERIES, LEGENDS, AND UNEXPLAINED PHENOMENA

MYSTERIES, LEGENDS, AND UNEXPLAINED PHENOMENA

MAGIC AND ALCHEMY

ROBERT M. PLACE

Consulting Editor: Rosemary Ellen Guiley

CHELSEA HOUSE
PUBLISHERS
An imprint of Infobase Publishing

MAGIC AND ALCHEMY

Chelsea House
An imprint of Infobase Publishing
132 West 31st Street
New York NY 10001

Library of Congress Cataloging-in-Publication Data

Place, Robert Michael.
  Magic and alchemy / Robert M. Place ; consulting editor, Rosemary Ellen Guiley.
    p. cm. — (Mysteries, legends, and unexplained phenomena)
  Includes bibliographical references and index.
  ISBN-13: 978-0-7910-9390-0 (hardcover : alk. paper)
  ISBN-10: 0-7910-9390-5 (hardcover : alk. paper) 1. Magic. 2. Alchemy. I. Guiley, Rosemary. II. Title.
  BF1621.P58 2009
  133.4'3—dc22

                              2009000676

Text design by James Scotto-Lavino
Cover design by Ben Peterson

Printed in the United States of America

Bang EJB 10 9 8 7 6 5 4 3 2 1

This book is printed on acid-free paper.

All links and Web addresses were checked and verified to be correct at the time of publication. Because of the dynamic nature of the Web, some addresses and links may have changed since publication and may no longer be valid.

Contents

Foreword

Did you ever have an experience that turned your whole world upside down? Maybe you saw a ghost or a UFO. Perhaps you had an unusual, vivid dream that seemed real. Maybe you suddenly knew that a certain event was going to happen in the future. Or, perhaps you saw a creature or a being that did not fit the description of anything known in the natural world. At first you might have thought your imagination was playing tricks on you. Then, perhaps, you wondered about what you experienced and went looking for an explanation.

Every day and night people have experiences they can't explain. For many people these events are life changing. Their comfort zone of what they can accept as "real" is put to the test. It takes only one such experience for people to question the reality of the mysterious worlds that might exist beyond the one we live in. Perhaps you haven't encountered the unknown, but you have an intense curiosity about it. Either way, by picking up this book, you've started an adventure to explore and learn more, and you've come to the right place! The book you hold has been written by a leading expert in the paranormal—someone who understands unusual experiences and who knows the answers to your questions.

As a seeker of knowledge, you have plenty of company. Mythology, folklore, and records of the past show that human beings have had paranormal experiences throughout history. Even prehistoric cave paintings and gravesites indicate that early humans had concepts of the supernatural and of an afterlife. Humans have always sought to understand paranormal experiences and to put them into a frame of reference that makes sense to us in our daily lives. Some of the greatest minds in history have grappled with questions about the paranormal. For example, Greek philosopher Plato pondered the nature of dreams and how we "travel" during them. Isaac Newton was interested in the esoteric study of alchemy, which has magical elements, and St. Thomas Aquinas explored the nature of angels and spirits. Philosopher William James joined organizations dedicated to psychical research; and even the inventor of the light bulb, Thomas Alva Edison, wanted to build a device that could talk to the dead. More recently, physicists such as David Bohm, Stephen Hawking, William Tiller, and Michio Kaku have developed ideas that may help explain how and why paranormal phenomena happen, and neuroscience researchers like Michael Persinger have explored the nature of consciousness.

Exactly what is a paranormal experience or phenomenon? "Para" is derived from a Latin term for "beyond." So "paranormal" means "beyond normal," or things that do not fit what we experience through our five senses alone and which do not follow the laws we observe in nature and in science. Paranormal experiences and phenomena run the gamut from the awesome and marvelous, such as angels and miracles, to the downright terrifying, such as vampires and werewolves.

Paranormal experiences have been consistent throughout the ages, but explanations of them have changed as societies, cultures, and technologies have changed. For example, our ancestors were much closer to the invisible realms. In times when life was simpler, they saw, felt, and experienced other realities on a daily basis. When night fell, the darkness was thick and quiet, and it was easier to see unusual things, such as ghosts. They had no electricity to keep the night lit up. They had no media for constant communication and entertainment. Travel was difficult. They had more time to notice subtle things that were just beyond their ordinary senses. Few doubted their experiences. They accepted the invisible realms as an extension of ordinary life.

Today, we have many distractions. We are constantly busy, from the time we wake up until we go to bed. The world is full of light and noise 24 hours a day, seven days a week. We have television, the Internet, computer games, and cell phones to keep us busy, busy, busy.

We are ruled by technology and science. Yet, we still have paranormal experiences very similar to those of our ancestors. Because these occurrences do not fit neatly into science and technology, many people think they are illusions, and there are plenty of skeptics always ready to debunk the paranormal and reinforce that idea.

In roughly the past 100 years, though, some scientists have studied the paranormal and attempted to find scientific evidence for it. Psychic phenomena have proven difficult to observe and measure according to scientific standards. However, lack of scientific proof does not mean paranormal experiences do not happen. Courageous scientists are still looking for bridges between science and the supernatural.

My personal experiences are behind my lifelong study of the paranormal. Like many children I had invisible playmates when I was very young, and I saw strange lights in the yard and woods that I instinctively knew were the nature spirits who lived there. Children seem to be very open to paranormal phenomena, but their ability to have these experiences often fades away as they become more involved in the outside world, or, perhaps, as adults tell them not to believe in what they experience, that it's only in their imagination. Even when I was very young, I was puzzled that other people would tell me with great authority that I did not experience what I knew I did.

A major reason for my interest in the paranormal is precognitive dreaming experienced by members of my family. Precognition means "fore knowing," or knowing the future. My mother had a lot of psychic experiences, including dreams of future events. As a teen it seemed amazing to me that dreams could show us the future. I was determined to learn more about this and to have such dreams myself. I found books that explained extrasensory perception, the knowing of information beyond the five senses. I learned about dreams and experimented with them. I taught myself to visit distant places in my dreams and to notice details about them that I could later verify in the physical world. I learned how to send people telepathic messages in dreams and how to receive messages in dreams. Every night became an exciting adventure.

Those interests led me to other areas of the paranormal. Pretty soon I was engrossed in studying all kinds of topics. I learned different techniques for divination, including the Tarot. I learned how to meditate. I took courses to develop my own psychic skills, and I gave psychic readings to others. Everyone has at least some natural psychic ability and can improve it with attention and practice.

Next I turned my attention to the skies, to ufology, and what might be "out there" in space. I studied the lore of angels and fairies. I delved into the dark shadowy realm of demons and monsters. I learned the principles of real magic and spell casting. I undertook investigations of haunted places. I learned how to see auras and do energy healing. I even participated in some formal scientific laboratory experiments for telepathy.

My studies led me to have many kinds of experiences that have enriched my understanding of the paranormal. I cannot say that I can prove anything in scientific terms. It may be some time yet before science and the paranormal stop flirting with each other and really get together. Meanwhile, we can still learn a great deal from our personal experiences. At the very least, our paranormal experiences contribute to our inner wisdom. I encourage others to do the same as I do. Look first for natural explanations of strange phenomena. If natural explanations cannot be found or seem unlikely, consider paranormal explanations. Many paranormal experiences fall into a vague area, where although natural causes might exist, we simply don't know what could explain them. In that case I tell people to trust their intuition that they had a paranormal experience. Sometimes the explanation makes itself known later on.

I have concluded from my studies and experiences that invisible dimensions are layered upon our world, and that many paranormal experiences occur when there are openings between worlds. The doorways often open at unexpected times. You take a trip, visit a haunted place, or have a strange dream—and suddenly reality shifts. You get a glimpse behind the curtain that separates the ordinary from the extraordinary.

The books in this series will introduce you to these exciting and mysterious subjects. You'll learn many things that will astonish you. You'll be given lots of tips for how to explore the paranormal on your own. Paranormal investigation is a popular field, and you don't have to be a scientist or a full-time researcher to explore it. There are many things you can do in your free time. The knowledge you gain from these books will help prepare you for any unusual and unexpected experiences.

As you go deeper into your study of the paranormal, you may come up with new ideas for explanations. That's one of the appealing aspects of paranormal investigation—there is always room for bold ideas. So, keep an open and curious mind, and think big. Mysterious worlds are waiting for you!

—Rosemary Ellen Guiley

Introduction

The word **magic** brings many ideas to mind. It may evoke the image of a Native American **shaman** dancing to bring a rainstorm to nurture his or her tribe's crops or an ancient Egyptian priest inscribing magical hieroglyphs on a mummy case to assure the deceased's success in the afterlife. It may suggest a medieval sorcerer standing in a circle drawn on the ground while he inscribes bits of Latin verse on the rim in hopes of summoning a creature from the unseen world or an alchemist observing a strange light forming in his or her flask. It may also bring to mind a fairy-tale witch who turns princes into frogs or a tuxedoed stage performer who pulls a rabbit out of a top hat.

Of course stage magicians are not actually performing the miracles that they appear to be. They use sleight-of-hand or trickery to create the illusion that magical things are happening. Similarly, the authors of myths and fairy tales can describe almost any magical event that then comes to life in the imaginations of those who hear it. Again, this is a type of illusion, one that is often illustrated by artists or filmmakers. This book is not about illusion. It is about the first examples, in which men or women attempt to create changes in physical reality using only their mental powers or mystical forces. The fact that magic works with unseen or hidden powers and is practiced by a select few who seem to have access to secret knowledge, explains why the study of magic may also be labeled the study of the occult, which means hidden or secret.

Although magic is not mere fantasy, it is dependent on imagination. Magical thinking depends on believing that imagination can be as real as physical reality. It is the conscious focusing of imagination on one's goals that empowers magic. This power is occult primarily because this mental discipline is difficult for most people to achieve. Magic can be called "the technology of imagination."

MAGIC, RELIGION, AND SCIENCE

Magic can be a troublesome term to define. *Merriam Webster's Collegiate Dictionary* explains that the term magic is derived from the Greek word *magus*. The Greeks borrowed this word from Persia where it was the name of a member of the priestly class, who were noted for performing magical rites. This brings up the first essential problem in defining magic: Is it separate from or connected to religion? On one hand, some modern religions, such as Christianity and Islam, condemn magic as an evil practice. On the other hand, prehistoric shamanistic magical practices and the state of spiritual awareness that they created seem to be the origin of religion. Even in modern times it is hard to separate religious thinking from magical thinking. For example, what is the essential difference between a magician using a magic charm to heal his patient or a priest using the relic of a saint for the same purpose?

The definition goes on to explain magic as, "the use of means (as charms or spells) believed to have supernatural power over natural forces."[1] This would seem to fit most people's idea of magic, but this definition contains the disclaimer "believed." This brings up the second essential problem. Modern science views magic as a superstition. This is in spite of the fact that magic, especially in the form of **alchemy,** is the ancestor of science and an accepted part of ancient Western culture. Also, many people in the West today and in other parts of the world continue to believe in and practice magic.

Most scientific or anthropological studies of modern magical and religious thought start with a discussion of the theories of Scottish folklorist and author, Sir James Frazer (1854–1941). Frazer documented similar magical and religious beliefs found in many diverse cultures around the world in *The Golden Bough: A Study in Magic and Religion,* published in 1890. He also used this book to advance a theory of cultural evolution, which placed magic on the bottom rung of an evolutionary ladder. Frazer's theory became a major influence on modern thinking.

Frazer's theory states that humans, finding themselves helpless in nature, first attempted to control nature with magic; in other words they put their trust in shamanism. As culture advanced, humans realized that magic is ineffective, abandoned it, and developed a belief in a higher power outside of their control, which they attempted to appease. Frazer calls this religion. When humans attained sufficient knowledge of the real workings of the world, Frazer continues, they abandoned this second "superstition" and entered into the practice of science. In this final stage, Frazer feels that the culture as a whole aims at real power over nature through science, although some individuals still cling to superstition.

Modern anthropologists have found a problem with Frazer's theory: Their observations do not support its neat sequential structure. Most primitive people believe in a higher power or powers and use both magic and technology or science in conjunction with this religious belief. The same is true of prehistoric peoples, ancient Greeks, or modern Americans. After all, shamanism is enjoying a resurgence in modern Western culture, even among people who value science.

The distinction between magic and religion seems to be found only in Western culture from the Middle Ages to the present. At the ancient roots of Western culture not only is there no distinction between magic and religion but science also seems to be combined with them. Most historians trace the origins of rational scientific thought in the West to the philosophers of the pre-Classical world, such as Pythagoras (c.580–572–c.500–490 B.C.E.) and his follower Empedocles (490–430 B.C.E.). Pythagoras is considered a philosopher and a mathematician and Empedocles is the creator of the rational discipline and investigation of physical reality that led to physics.

Pythagoras' view that all reality can be expressed in numbers is one of the most important root concepts in Western science. Yet,

Pythagoras was the founder of a mystical religious movement that included mathematical speculations about the universe, beliefs in reincarnation, and ideas about the spiritual evolution of humans toward a godlike state of higher consciousness. Likewise, Empedocles, who was a member of that movement, wrote his theories on the nature of physical reality in the form of poetry and would have called himself a magician. Empedocles' theories about the four elements became the basis of alchemy, which evolved into modern science. Pythagoras, Empedocles, and other Pythagorean philosophers seem to be responsible for initiating a religious, scientific, and magical synthesis that is the root of modern Western culture and led to modern science and technology.

St. Augustine (354–430) was an influential theologian who lived in the twilight of the Classical Age and helped to create the medieval Christian worldview. He described magic as a continuation of pagan culture and therefore unchristian. His view persisted until, by the end of the Middle Ages, magic was considered a heresy and subject to censorship or punishment by the Inquisition. This happened in spite of the fact that the essence of the Christian mass is the magical transformation of the bread and wine on the altar into the body and blood of Christ; that all saints were reported to have performed miracles; and that many Christians—including popes—were involved in alchemy, which was considered white magic. In order to think of magic as evil and unchristian, it was necessary to see it as something separate from religion and redefine sanctioned magic as something else, for example, a miracle. Although anthropologists do not find this separation in cultures other than those influenced by the Bible, it continues to influence modern Western scientific thinking. Today scientists think of magic not as evil but as an ignorant superstition; most are not as quick to view religion in the same light.

Magic, however, is not simply primitive technology, unchristian, or superstition. It is the origin of both religion and science and has some qualities of each but not entirely of either one. It is a field of study that lies between the two. This may be one reason why both religion and science reject magic, but it may also be magic's power. It resolves the differences between religion and science and can lead to a personal spiritual experience that is in some way verifiable.

THE PSYCHOLOGY OF MAGIC

Today attitudes toward magic are changing. Not all scientists continue to share a negative view of magic. Modern anthropologists have been setting the record straight about magic's role in cultural evolution. Perhaps the strongest support for the validity of magic, however, has come from psychologists, particularly the work of Carl G. Jung (1875–1961), the famous Swiss founder of depth psychology, which examines the unconscious.

Jung observed that often coincidences would happen in everyday life that seemed magical or dreamlike. For example, Jung was talking to a patient about the symbolism of the Egyptian scarab beetle while he was looking out the window of his office; at that exact moment a large beetle walked across the glass in front of him. In another example, he had a dream about a kingfisher, a bird that is rare in Switzerland, and the next morning one washed up on the shore of the lake by his home. This had never happened before and did not happen again after that morning. Ancient peoples would have considered these events magical and possibly messages from the gods. Jung decided to create a new scientific term for these events. He combined *syn*, which means "together," with *chron*, which means "time." And then added *icity* on the end to make it into a noun. The resulting term was **synchronicity**.

Jung defines a synchronicity as an event happening in the physical world that coincides with an event happening in our minds, together in time, in a way that the mind feels that it is magically meaningful. Jung felt that nothing causes this to happen; it happens simply because the outer world of physical reality and the inner world of the mind are connected. In other words, imagination and physical reality share a connection. It is a short step from this realization to wanting to experiment to find out what effect one's imagination has on reality.

Most religious philosophies teach that there is a connection between the mind and outer reality. The Bible tells that people reap what they sow. This means that one's thoughts and actions determine the quality of one's life. In the Buddhist sutras this principle is stated even more directly. Buddha taught that one's thoughts create the world. Jung verified this philosophical observation through psychology. He found that his patient's mental state did determine the quality of his or her life and could cause changes in their physical health and even in their outer circumstances. He developed a technique in which his patients could work directly with the symbols that they found in their unconscious to help heal their minds and improve their lives. He called this technique **active imagination**. Again, it seems that he was inventing a scientific term to describe magic.

In active imagination a person calls up an internal symbol in his or her imagination and interacts or has a conversation with it. A symbol is an image that naturally comes into the conscious mind from the unconscious part the way that images appear in dreams, but in this case one is calling it up while awake. The symbol can take the form of an object, an animal, or a human and can even appear as an angel or a **demon** like the ones summoned by magicians. The skill of active imagination lies in being able to let the symbol speak and act for itself instead of putting words into its mouth or controlling its actions through wishful thinking.

Jung found that active imagination was the most effective technique he had for making changes in the minds of his patients and quickly bringing them to a healthier state. As patients spoke with the inner symbols and made improvements in their relationship with these inner aspects of their personality, changes happened in their lives. They even found that other people began to treat them differently and their relationships and physical circumstances improved. Lucky breaks and beneficial chance encounters just seemed to happen once their minds were in a receptive state.

Like Jung was using this inner technique to create desirable changes in his patient's life, the magician is looking for changes in his or her life. The magician may want to become healthier, richer, happier, or more powerful. It is this inner dialogue and the changes that it produces in the mind that allows the outer changes to happen and this inner dialogue is the true object of magic. The magician evolves spiritually as he or she comes to a realization of how his or her thoughts create the world.

BLACK AND WHITE

Traditionally, magic is divided into two types, categorized as white magic and black magic, also known as sorcery. These categories are also referred to as high magic and low magic. White or high magic is a practice that is intended to do good or to bring the practitioner to a higher spiritual state, referred to as enlightenment or cosmic consciousness. Black or low magic, on the other hand, is magic used to obtain the practitioner's physical desires at the expense of others. Alchemy is generally considered a form of white magic because the alchemist intends to alter his or her consciousness through the work and become an enlightened sage. Even in this field, however, there were alchemists called **puffers**, because of their impatient use of their bellows to stoke their fires; they were only interested in getting rich by turning lead into gold.

Often it is hard to determine if a magical practice is white or black. Obviously if a magician summons a demon to harm an enemy this would fit everyone's definition of black magic. Another magician may consider himself or herself a white practitioner and summon an angel to do harm to someone he or she considers evil. In essence there is no difference between these actions; after all, in biblical religions demons are considered to be only fallen or harmful angels. Also, if a magician uses magic to obtain his or her physical desires but in the process comes to realize that it is accomplished by changing his or her thoughts then they are simultaneously achieving the highest goal of white magic. Folk magic, as practiced by common people, is also often categorized as low magic. **Ceremonial magic**, which involves the use of expensive props and is, therefore, generally practiced by upper-class magicians, is classified as high magic. This is a class prejudice.

A more realistic approach would be to categorize magic as high or low by determining how the magician is trying to attain his or her goal. If the magician's goal is accomplished by becoming healthier in his or her mind and changing his or her actions and thoughts, it would be high magic. If he or she is trying to reach a goal by manipulating others, it would be low magic. In this view any magic that is intended to attain a goal by harming another or even by manipulating another in a seemingly positive way is considered low magic. The highest magic is the practice that brings one to the realization that the physical world and the inner world of the mind share a connection, and it is through this connection that one can attain any desire, including the desire to be at one with the world.

WHAT THIS BOOK COVERS

This book is not intended to turn anyone into a magician or an alchemist but the information here may help. Although magic and alchemy have been practiced since prehistoric times in most cultures and parts of the world, some of this history is covered in *Shamanism*, another book in the Mysteries, Legends, and Unexplained Phenomena series. This book primarily focuses on magic and alchemy as practiced in the Western historic tradition. Other than brief mentions, it does not cover **astrology**, **divination**, or witchcraft, even though those things are part of this tradition, because those topics are covered in detail in other volumes of this series. This book discusses the history of magic and alchemy from the ancient world to modern New Age practices. It covers the basic concepts of magic and alchemy, the tools of the magician and the alchemist, and the practice of the magic ritual and the alchemical Great Work.

It also discusses the mystical philosophy that is shared by magic and alchemy. This philosophy originated in ancient Egypt and was attributed to the teachings of a god. It was designed to bring one to a mystical state of awareness and although kept in the background of Western culture it has been a continuing influence since its inception.

The Beginning of Magic

The year is 131 B.C.E. and the descendants of the Greek general Ptolemy rule Egypt from the Hellenistic city of Alexandria. Like all educated Alexandrians, Hui speaks Greek but when it comes to his religious beliefs he is thoroughly Egyptian and can look back on a 3000-year spiritual tradition. It is not surprising, therefore, that in times of trouble he turns to the ancient gods of his people and to magic to make things right. Hui has an infection that is not responding to the medicines prescribed by the healer, and Hui blames this misfortune on the demon Apep, a monstrous serpent that is the enemy of the sun god, Ra. Therefore, he has decided to use magic to protect him from the demon.

Hui picks a lucky day from the calendar for his ritual. On that day, he rises before dawn, bathes, and dresses in white linen. Then he enters the ritual space outside of his house where he would normally pray to the rising sun. Sunrise is the most powerful time of the day, and Hui wants to make use of this power to help his magic. Following the directions in *The Book of Overthrowing Apep*, Hui draws a serpent in green paint on a clean piece of papyrus and covers the figure in wax, which he sculpted to the shape of the serpent. After engraving Apep's name into the serpent and inlaying the lines with green, Hui builds a small fire and places the wax figure in the flames.

As the serpent burns, Hui recites the **words of power** from the text. Starting with, "Fire be upon thee Apep, thou enemy of Ra," he

Figure 1.1 *Apep's name is written on its body in Greek in this artist's depiction. Below, Apep's name appears in hieroglyphics.* (Robert M. Place)

continues to the last lines, which read, "Ra triumphs over Apep. Taste thou death Apep." To seal the power of this final declaration, Hui recites it while facing the rising sun in the east, repeats the last lines again while facing south, then again while facing west, and one final time while facing north.

IN THE BEGINNING

There have always been people with special powers that others look up to or go to for help. These men and women exist in all traditional tribal cultures and anthropologists, the scientists who study culture, have labeled them shamans. At times people have also called them witch doctors, medicine men, **sorcerers**, witches, or even magicians.

Anthropological evidence suggests that prehistoric shamans practiced magic in the caves of southwestern Europe 40,000 years ago, and it is likely that the practice is older than that. Magic, therefore, is likely to be as old as the human·race.

Most prehistoric shamans were concerned with using magic to help with the success of the hunt. They painted pictures on the walls of caves of the types of animals that the hunters desired. It is believed that this practice was a type of **sympathetic magic**, based on the idea that like attracts like. By painting a picture of a deer or a bison, the prehistoric shaman hoped to draw the actual animal to the hunter. Perhaps he or she believed that the picture captured the animal's soul and that the body would follow.

By observing the practices of shamans in tribal cultures that still exist, researchers have learned more about the practices of these ancient magicians. To perform his or her magic a shaman prepared a ritual space. Often the space was circular, but it was most important that its relation to the four directions, north, south, east, and west, were clearly indicated and that the sacred space in the center was obvious. Next the shaman used the repetitive sound of a drum or a rattle to enter a trance and go on an inner journey. Using the sacred center as a place for the mind to enter, he or she would go to a land that few people are familiar with. This place was a strange, dreamlike world of the imagination. The details and structure of this world are similar in the reports of shamans from different times and places. Journeying to this world was something like entering a dream while awake and being able to decide what to do there. The world is normally invisible, but to a shaman in a trance it was just as real as the physical world.

While on a journey, the shaman would meet gods, ghosts, spirits, or animal helpers and gather magical power. To the shaman the spirits and helpers are neither good nor evil. Even harmful spirits, such as the spirits that cause disease, or the ghosts of the dead, could become valuable allies that would help to cure illness. Once the shaman gained this power and formed alliances with spirits, he or she would be able to make changes in the everyday visible world, such as healing the sick or making it rain. The shaman's allies could then empower potions or medicines made of herbs or carvings or drawings of the spirits that served as magical **talismans**. Here is a list of the kinds of things that shamans were, and in modern tribal cultures still are, called on to do:

1 To cure illnesses

2 To find game for the hunt

3 To divine the future

4 To interpret dreams

5 To find lost people or objects

6 To help guide the tribe

7 To appease spirits

8 To control weather, especially when rain is needed

9 To help people feel good

About 10,000 years ago humans entered the Neolithic, or New Stone Age, period. Instead of living in small groups and relying on hunting and gathering for food, many humans began to raise animals and crops on farms and they stored food in shelters—ready to eat as they needed it. Then larger groups of people could live together in villages. Shamans adapted to these changes and added magical skills to their practice that addressed the needs of the new groups. These included performing rituals for weather magic, helping the crops, performing group healing, or healing animals.

In the Neolithic period, however, a new type of religion formed based on the needs of the village. People started to perform group rituals guided by priests. Priests were the first alternative to the shamans, and sometimes they were rivals for authority. In contrast to the intuitive spontaneous visions of the shamans, the priests worshiped specific gods and told stories about them called myths, which remained basically the same over time. The type of magic that the priests practiced made use of elaborate props and clothing and formal ceremonies that called on the gods for aid and helped people to identify with the gods and their myths. This was the beginning of ceremonial magic.

As the first civilizations developed, the roles of priests and shamans sometimes merged or became confused. In addition to priests, professional magicians appeared. They performed ceremonial magic or prepared charms for a fee. This professional practice coexisted with traditions of folk magic that may have had roots in shamanism. Magic in all of these forms existed in every culture in the world. Discussing all of these branches falls beyond the limits of this book. Therefore, this book focuses on the Western tradition, starting with the cradles of Western civilization in the Middle East. There is a large body of ancient Egyptian texts that have been discovered, which discuss magical practices, and there is a direct link between these and later European practices.

EGYPTIAN MAGIC

In 3150 B.C.E. Egyptian civilization bloomed in the fertile valley created by the Nile River in the North African desert. Because of the protection provided by the surrounding desert and the natural rhythm of the Nile, which flooded its banks yearly and renewed the fertility of the fields, Egyptian culture and religion remained stable for more than 3,000 years. In Egypt magic and religion were inseparable. Their priests were famous throughout the ancient world as gifted and wise magicians.

Ancient texts describe Egyptian magicians performing miracles that rival the feats of Moses in the Bible. Over 2,000 years before Moses was said to part the Red Sea, the Egyptian priest Tchatcha-em-ankh was said to have parted the waters of a lake and for no more exalted reason than to retrieve a piece of jewelry.[1] Other texts tell of magicians cutting the head off a goose and then restoring it to life or resurrecting a dead man to hear his testimony in a trial.[2] Even today Egyptian magic and religion fascinates modern New Age mystics.

One of the main concerns of Egyptian magic and religion was to guarantee that there would be life after death, which may be considered the ultimate goal of all white magic. In the myth of Osiris, one of the most important of the Egyptian gods and one of the world's oldest known gods, he was said to have returned from the dead. By identifying with Osiris and learning from his story every Egyptian hoped to do the same. In comparing Osiris' role to that of Christ's, who also rose from the dead, in Christianity, it becomes clear how important Osiris was to ancient Egyptians. He was their role model, the same way that Christ is the role model for all Christians. Osiris' myth is also filled with descriptions of magic.

THE MYTH OF OSIRIS

Osiris was said to have ruled Egypt in the distant past as pharaoh, the Egyptian name for a king. For his queen Osiris chose his beautiful sister Isis, who was as wise as she was beautiful and gifted at magic. Osiris was an excellent pharaoh. He taught the Egyptians art, law, and civilized ways of farming and building, and his subjects loved him. His vizier and scribe, the god Thoth, who had a human body and the head of a wading bird called an ibis, taught the people a type of magical writing with pictures called hieroglyphs. He also taught them magic and other arts and sciences and recorded all of his teachings in the first book, called *The Book of Thoth*. As the god of magic and writing, Thoth was the master of "words of power," the words that gave power to a magic spell.

Osiris also had a brother, Set, who was evil and jealous of Osiris' abilities and popularity. Because he was jealous, Set decided to kill Osiris. To accomplish this he had a beautiful box made to the exact shape and size of Osiris' body and invited his brother, many of their friends, and 72 evil accomplices, to a feast. At the banquet Set declared that he would award the beautifully crafted box to the person who fit in it the best. All of the guests took turns lying in the box, but of course, it only fit Osiris. No sooner had Osiris lain down in the box than Set and his accomplices slammed down the lid and nailed the box shut. Then they carried the box to the Nile and threw it in the river. As the box floated away, water seeped in and Osiris drowned. The box traveled out to sea and eventually landed on the shore of Byblos, an ancient city that was on the shore of what is now Lebanon but was then called Phoenicia. There, a large tamarisk tree grew over it and encased the box in its trunk.

When Isis learned that her husband was dead, she went into mourning but she also used her magic to divine the location of the box. Isis found that the king of Phoenicia had cut down the tamarisk tree and used the trunk, containing the box and Osiris, as the main pillar in his palace. Isis went to Phoenicia and befriended the queen, who let her remove the box from the pillar. Then she returned home with the body of her husband, but once again Set intervened. He found the body of Osiris, cut it into 14 pieces, and scattered them over Egypt.

Again Isis used her magic, this time to find the parts of Osiris. She found all of the parts except one but that did not discourage her. She made a replacement part out of gold and put Osiris back together by wrapping him tightly with linen like a mummy. Then with the help of Thoth and his words of power, she brought Osiris back to life. Isis then mated with him and gave birth to their son Horus, a god of the sun and moon, depicted with the head of a falcon. Osiris was proud of Horus and decided to let him take over ruling the land of the living. Osiris chose instead to become the god of the dead, where he would preside over the judgment of the soul of each person in the afterlife. Horus, meanwhile, battled Set and avenged his father.

THE PARTS OF THE SOUL

It is well known that the Egyptians mummified their dead, wrapped them in linen, and placed them in boxes carved in their likeness. These were magical acts connected to the myth of Osiris. By doing these things, the Egyptians believed that they were imitating Osiris.

Figure 1.2 *Thoth* (left) *and the goddess Isis* (right) *use words of power to resurrect Osiris. Seen in the center, Osiris is wrapped like a mummy except for his arms, which hold the symbols of authority. On his head he wears the white crown of Upper Egypt. His skin is green to symbolize regeneration and his connection to the vegetable kingdom.* (Robert M. Place)

They wanted to preserve their bodies because they believed that their souls had several distinct parts and some parts would need the body even after they were dead. The three principle parts of the soul were the Ka, which represented the physical needs of the body and would stay close to the body after death; the Ba, which had mind and will and could wander the earth after death but needed to return to body; and the Akh, which did not need the body and could become one with the immortal celestial world.

Each soul part had a symbolic image that was its hieroglyph but that was also used in magical talismans designed to protect or direct

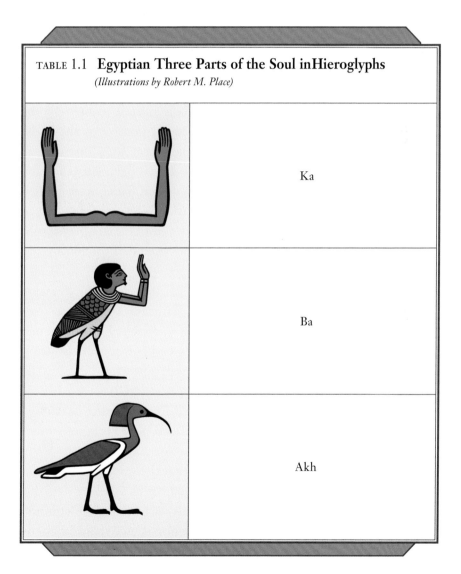

TABLE 1.1 **Egyptian Three Parts of the Soul in Hieroglyphs**
(Illustrations by Robert M. Place)

	Ka
	Ba
	Akh

the soul. Table 1.1 depicts the hieroglyphs for each soul part. The Ka is depicted as upraised human arms, the Ba as a human-headed hawk, and the Akh as a crested ibis.

TALISMANS, WORDS OF POWER, AND MAGICAL ART

The body was carefully preserved and wrapped to satisfy the needs of the first two parts of the soul. To be doubly sure that it was protected, magical talismans or **amulets** made of precious stones or ceramic were woven into the wrappings. There were two kinds of talismans. Some were representations of the gods or symbols related to hieroglyphs that were designed to represent the beneficial powers of the gods. Others were images of body parts or organs that were intended as magical replacements in case of loss of the actual part. All talismans were activated through the use of words of power, which were spoken ritually over them but also inscribed on the objects, making use of the magical hieroglyphs. Words of power were often taken right from the story of Osiris and other gods and were intended to identify the talisman with the story.

Related to words of power was another magical device: magic names. The Egyptians believed that the name of a person, a god, or another lesser spirit was intimately tied to the soul of that being. Through magic, a name could be used to extend power over the being it belonged to, human or otherwise. The more powerful the being the more power the name commanded. The creator god, Nesi-Amsu, was said to have brought himself and the world into existence by simply saying his name. Because their names were so powerful, gods often kept them secret.

In the myth of Ra and Isis, it was said that the great and powerful sun god, Ra, was one who jealously guarded his name. Desiring this power, Isis used her magic to create a deadly serpent and left it in the path of the sun god to be sure it would bite him. Once stricken by the serpent, Ra could only be saved by Isis, but before she helped him, she demanded knowledge of his secret name. Equipped with this name, Isis became one of the most powerful magicians.

Magical names were often inscribed on objects as a type of word of power. In *The Book of the Dead*, a book written for the deceased and enclosed in the tomb with him or her, magic names, as words of power, were provided for all the spirits one was likely meet in the afterlife. This was to help the deceased command the spirits and continue on his or her journey. Also, as in the story of Hui, by inscribing the name Apep on the wax snake Hui empowered the image and used it to destroy Apep's influence over him.

Besides preserving the body, Egyptian priests used magical art to provide physical comforts for the deceased in the afterlife. Egyptians were awed by the power of art to imitate nature. They felt that, through magic, sculpted or painted images of food would turn into real food for the Ka and the Ba of the deceased. They also provided sculptures or paintings of livestock, fields of crops, and workers to tend the animals and cultivate the fields. All of these works of art were created to magically come to life for the deceased and provide the comforts that he or she had enjoyed before death. It seems that the Egyptians believed that you could take it with you when you died.

MAGIC RITUALS

All of the works of art found in Egyptian tombs and temples are essentially magical. All of them had to be empowered through magic rituals. Rituals, however, were also created to directly cause magical effects, and magical objects were made to serve in these rituals. All rituals depend on the creation of a magical or sacred space that needs to be oriented toward the four cardinal directions: north, south, east, and west. Evidence of this exists in the famous great pyramids of Egypt, which have a square base with four triangular sides. Modern research has confirmed that the great pyramids are deliberately and accurately aligned with the cardinal directions. Essentially, a pyramid is a symbolic mountain that functions as the sacred center of the world and symbolizes the joining of heaven and earth. It is believed to have represented to the Egyptians the mythological primordial mound from which the earth was created.

Considering the importance placed on the sun, particularly the moments of sunrise and sunset as sacred times, it is not surprising that Egyptians were keenly aware of the east, where the sun rose, the west, where the sun set, and the north and the south which formed the perpendicular axes. Most of their sacred structures reflect this awareness in both alignment and symbolism. Isis' son, Horus, who was the god of both the sun and the moon, had four sons of his own, who represented the four cardinal directions. Each had the head of a different creature, and each was associated with organs of the body and with a goddess as shown in Table 1.2.

The Egyptians used the symbolism of the four sons and the four goddesses to orientate magical structures to the cardinal directions. In numerous tombs the vital organs of a mummy were removed and placed in jars, each sculpted with the appropriate head of the son who protected those organs. These jars were arranged in square

TABLE 1.2 The Four Sons of Horus and Their Correlations

SON OF HORUS	IMAGE	ORGANS	GODDESS	DIRECTION
Mestha	Man-headed	Stomach, Large Intestines	Isis	South
Hapi	Dog-headed	Small Intestines	Nephthys	North
Tuamutef	Jackal-headed	Lungs, Heart	Neith	East
Qebhsennuf	Hawk-headed	Liver, Gall Bladder	Serqet	West

Figure 1.3   *The deceased is resurrected from the casket amid the four sons of Horus. From left to right, the sons are Hapi, Mestha, Tuamutef, and Qebhsennuf.* (Robert M. Place)

formation to align them to the directions. Also, the figures of the four goddesses were used to orient rectangular or square boxes or structures to the four directions, effectively turning them into a sacred shrine.

Egyptian priests performed numerous rituals. Their practice is considered the oldest known ceremonial magic. One of the most important rituals was called the "opening of the mouth." In this ritual the magician priest would magically empower the deceased to be able to speak in the afterlife. This was considered the most important ritual to aid the deceased, because without it he or she would not be able to use the words of power provided in *The Book of the Dead*. Figure 1.4 is a drawing based on an Egyptian scroll painting that depicts this ritual. The magician priest is wearing a ritual garment made of leopard skin and using a magic wand, called an **urhekau**, with the head of a serpent carved at its tip. In an act of sympathetic magic, the priest is directing the wand toward a statue of the deceased. By working the magic on the statue he hopes to cause the same effect to happen to the body of the deceased.

Figure 1.4 *A magician priest* (right) *performs the opening of the mouth ritual.* (Robert M. Place)

MAGIC IN EVERYDAY LIFE

Because most Egyptian art and literature known today comes from tombs, it may seem that the Egyptians were unduly concerned with death and the afterlife. Although tombs are ideal places for preserving artifacts, not all evidence of Egyptian civilization comes from them. Even in tombs, however, Egyptian art and writing illustrates the vibrant culture of the living. Even as magic was behind every aspect of funeral art, magic was also inseparable from everyday life.

The Egyptians, like all ancient people, saw the world as inhabited by a multitude of invisible beings. Some of these were beneficial gods, but the world was also inhabited by mobs of harmful or malevolent beings, that caused injury, illness, and destruction. These malevolent beings are called demons. Mostly they took the form of monstrous

The Curse of Tutankhamun

In November 1922 archeologist Howard Carter (1874–1939) discovered one of the best-preserved tombs in the Egyptian desert. It was the tomb of the boy pharaoh Tutankhamun, who had died in 1323 B.C.E. In February 1923 he opened the burial chamber and made one of the most important discoveries of the century. The chamber was filled with dazzlingly beautiful ancient art that quickly captured the public imagination. By April of the same year romance novelist Marie Corelli wrote a letter to the *New York World* newspaper warning Carter and his team that they faced "dire punishment" for disturbing the tomb. She claimed that the ancient Egyptians had placed magical curses on anyone who would rob their tombs and that these curses were backed by secret poisons that were enclosed in the artifacts in such a way that anyone who opened them would suffer the consequences.

Only two weeks after this letter appeared, Lord Carnarvon, the financial backer of the expedition, died from a mosquito bite that had become infected after being nicked with a razor by a barber. The unlikely circumstances that led to Carnarvon's death following so quickly after the publication of Corelli's letter seemed to affirm the accuracy of her claim. The newspapers seized on the story and the "curse of Tutankhamun" was repeated so often people started to accept it as a fact.

The facts, however, are that there is no archeological evidence to support the claim that the Egyptians used secret poisons in their tombs. Most ancient warnings addressed to tomb robbers focused on the damage that they were doing to their souls and did not make threats on their lives. In 1934 the curator of the Egyptology department at the Metropolitan Museum of Art decided to find out how the supposed curse had affected Carter's team. He found that of the 26 people who had been present at the opening of the tomb six had died and the rest were still alive at that time—not an impressive death toll for a curse. Carter, who should have been most affected by the curse, lived another 17 years after the opening. Carnarvon's daughter, who was also at the opening, was alive and well at the anniversary celebration of the discovery in 1972.[3]

snakes, scorpions, or crocodiles, but they could also take human or apelike form.

Magic was the accepted way of undoing the harm caused by a demon or of protecting oneself from a demon. One of the most effective methods for undoing harm was a type of sympathetic magic in which one made an image of the demon and destroyed it, hoping to also destroy the demon or at least the demon's influence. This is similar to the ritual in the story of Hui at the beginning of this chapter. This magical device is also familiar today as a voodoo doll. Pins stuck into a voodoo doll are meant to cause pain or even death to one's enemy, who is usually human. Ancient Egyptians were not above using their magical images to cause pain for another person, but images could also be used for love magic and to heal others. Figure 1.4 shows that the priest could make use of a magic image for one of the most important and beneficial rituals.

In the belief that an ounce of protection is worth a pound of cure, most Egyptians preferred to use magic to protect themselves from demons or to attract the protection of a god. For this they turned to talismans of stone or ceramic, similar to those used to help the dead. It is believed that every Egyptian man, woman, and child wore one or more protective talismans daily in the form of jewelry.

In other cultures talismans fall into two categories. First there are those that make use of words written on parchment or engraved on a hard substance, such as quotes from the Koran or the Bible engraved on a silver pendant. Second there are those that make use of symbols or images, such as a carving of an elephant or a hand worn for luck. Because the Egyptians wrote with pictures, their talismans were based on these hieroglyphic images, and they fit both of these categories at the same time. This gave them a unique power in which words and images were combined. To add to this power each talisman had prescribed stones or colors that were recommended for each image. Table 1.3 depicts six of the most common Egyptian talismans. Many of these images are familiar because they are still used in jewelry today.

TABLE 1.3 **Common Egyptian Talismans** *(Illustrations by Robert M. Place)*	
	**Utchat:** This was the most common talisman. It is a representation of the eye of Horus. It can face either left or right to represent Horus' two eyes, which were said to be the sun and the moon. This talisman could be made of lapis lazuli, carnelian, granite, silver, gold, or wood. Egyptians wore it to bring them the blessings of Horus: strength, vigor, protection, safety, and good health.
	**Scarab:** This talisman was extremely popular and thousands of them have been uncovered. It represents the Egyptian dung beetle, which lays its eggs in a ball of dung and rolls it through the desert. The Egyptians likened its ball to the sun and the beetle became associated with Khepri, the god of the rising sun. It could be made of various green or blue stones or in ceramic or ivory. The Egyptians believed that the Scarab offered its wearer the life renewing power of the sun and the promise of life after death. It was often placed on mummies as protection or a substitute for the heart. Words of power can be inscribed on its underside.
	**Tyet:** This talisman represents the knot or buckle of the girdle of Isis. It can be made of any red stone, such as carnelian or jasper, or of red glass. It can also be made of gold. It symbolizes the blood and the words of power of Isis. Egyptians wore it so that the blood and the words of power of Isis would come to their protection. When worn by the dead it would give them access to every place in the underworld. To empower the Tyet it was bathed in an infusion of ankham flowers.

(continues)

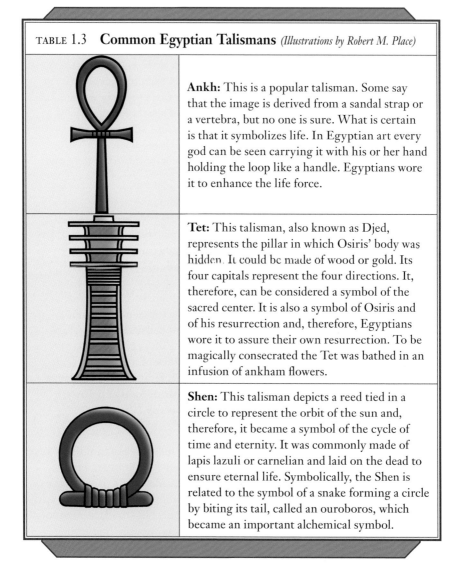

TABLE 1.3 **Common Egyptian Talismans** (*Illustrations by Robert M. Place*)

Ankh: This is a popular talisman. Some say that the image is derived from a sandal strap or a vertebra, but no one is sure. What is certain is that it symbolizes life. In Egyptian art every god can be seen carrying it with his or her hand holding the loop like a handle. Egyptians wore it to enhance the life force.

Tet: This talisman, also known as Djed, represents the pillar in which Osiris' body was hidden. It could be made of wood or gold. Its four capitals represent the four directions. It, therefore, can be considered a symbol of the sacred center. It is also a symbol of Osiris and of his resurrection and, therefore, Egyptians wore it to assure their own resurrection. To be magically consecrated the Tet was bathed in an infusion of ankham flowers.

Shen: This talisman depicts a reed tied in a circle to represent the orbit of the sun and, therefore, it became a symbol of the cycle of time and eternity. It was commonly made of lapis lazuli or carnelian and laid on the dead to ensure eternal life. Symbolically, the Shen is related to the symbol of a snake forming a circle by biting its tail, called an ouroboros, which became an important alchemical symbol.

The Philosophy of Magic

Lucian was a Greek living in Syria in the second century B.C.E. He had been a prosperous merchant for years but now his business was failing and he found himself falling into a deep depression. If he was a modern man, Lucian might have decided that he needed the help of a psychotherapist or even a financial advisor, but to him it seemed obvious that he was suffering the effects of a curse placed on him by one of his enemies. He, therefore, decided that a counter curse was the cure.

In the dark of night Lucian threw dill into his fire and summoned Hermes as the messenger and guide of the dead. He asked Hermes to carry his message to the underworld. Then with an iron stylus he inscribed his counter curse on a thin sheet of lead. He wrote: "If anyone has put a binding spell on me, as Hermes is my witness, I bind them in the terrifying name of the demon." Then he wrote the magical name of power. This was a name composed of the seven Greek vowels written in a triangle so that a single alpha was at the top, and below this epsilon was written twice, then below this eta was written three times, and the pattern continued with iota, omicron, and upsilon until at the base omega was written seven times. This name could only be pronounced by singing the seven notes of the scale and drawing each one out longer as the chant progressed (see next page). Afterward Lucian twisted the lead to activate the curse and went out and buried it in a cemetery.

A
E E
H H H
I I I I
O O O O O
Y Y Y Y Y
Ω Ω Ω Ω Ω Ω Ω

THE FERTILE CRESCENT

Many Western magicians, from the Renaissance to the present, have used Egypt as a model for their practice. Many other traditions from the Middle East also contributed to Western magical practice. The synthesis of these traditions took place in Alexandria, Egypt, in the first to the third centuries after the birth of Christ.

The Middle Eastern traditions stem from the ancient civilizations of the area known as the Fertile Crescent. This area stretches from the eastern Mediterranean coast that is now part of Syria, Lebanon, and Israel, to the fertile lands that exist between the Tigris and Euphrates Rivers as they flow to the Persian Gulf. To the ancient Greeks this eastern end was known as Mesopotamia and it is now part of Syria, Turkey, Iran, and Iraq. Unlike Egypt, with its insular and stable culture, the Fertile Crescent was inhabited by several cultures, which migrated, conquered, and merged over the centuries.

The first civilized people in this area were the Sumerians, who settled in the southern region of Mesopotamia about 6,000 to 7,000 years ago. The Sumerians had an advanced culture with distinctive arts and urban centers. Around 3500 B.C.E. they became the first people to develop writing and therefore the first to leave historic records. Another of their achievements was the construction of artificial mountains in the form of step pyramids called ziggurats, which they used to observe the sky and worship their gods who lived there.

In 2350 B.C.E. the Akkadians, the first Semitic people (people who spoke a Semitic language, which is related to modern Hebrew and

Arabic) in this area, conquered the Sumerians and created an empire between the Tigris and the Euphrates rivers. Eventually their language dominated the region, but they also adopted many aspects of Sumerian culture, including cuneiform writing, ziggurats, and sky watching. The Akkadians created the oldest written astrological text. From 1792–1750 B.C.E. the famous Babylonian ruler Hammurabi unified the area. After that, Babylonian culture, synthesized with the earlier cultures, became dominant in Mesopotamia.

During this period, sometime between 2000 and 1825 B.C.E., the patriarch of the Hebrew people, Abraham, left the Babylonian city of Ur and brought his people to the other end of the Fertile Crescent, to what is now Israel. There they founded a religion that focused on their one tribal god to the exclusion of all others. This was the beginning of the monotheistic biblical tradition that led to the creation of Judaism, Christianity, and Islam.

DEMONS

Like the Egyptians, the Babylonians believed that the world was inhabited by hosts of unseen creatures, such as demons, that were responsible for disease and suffering. They used magic to protect themselves from these malevolent influences. Babylonian demons could take the shape of snakes, donkeys, vicious dogs, lions, or even a formless mist or void. They tended to inhabit graveyards, caves, ruins, and deserts, especially at night. Compared to the Egyptians, though, the Babylonians were at a disadvantage in their struggle with evil because their gods were not necessarily helpful. The Babylonians believed that humans were created from the body of a fallen god or demon and that the gods looked on them as their slaves. As a result, they lived in fear of offending their gods by breaking a divine rule or not properly conducting the rituals designed to appease them. Misfortune, therefore, could just as easily come from an angry god as from a demon.

The first rule of magical protection in Babylon was to stay on the good side of the gods by conscientiously performing ceremonies to

Figure 2.1 *A Babylonian lion-headed demon caused illness.* (Ernest Lehner, *Symbols, Signs, and Signets* [1950])

honor them and observing magical taboos to avoid falling into sin. Once the favor of the gods was established, Babylonians could protect themselves from demons by wearing talismans sculpted in the likeness of a god. These were made of the proper stone and attached with the appropriate-colored thread. Like the Egyptians, Babylonians could make an image of the demon and destroy it or let it drift away on the river in a small boat. If all went well the gods would send a guardian spirit to help. The spirits were something like a guardian angel.

In the sixth century B.C.E. the Persians conquered Mesopotamia and created the largest empire the world had known up until that time. Known as the Achaemenid Empire, it came to include Persia, the entire Fertile Crescent, Turkey, and Egypt, and it tried, unsuccessfully, to include Greece. The Persian religion was founded by the prophet Zoroaster, or as he is known in Persia, Zarathushtra. He is thought to have lived in the sixth century B.C.E. He viewed the world as an arena of battle between two gods: Ahura Mazda, the king of light and god of goodness, and Ahriman, the prince of darkness and god of evil. Ahura Mazda commanded six archangels, who in turn each commanded an army of angels and Ahriman, to keep things even, commanded six archdemons, who in turn each commanded an army of demons. Humans were asked to come to the aid of Ahura Mazda by promoting good.

Zoroastrianism also gave birth to a complex system of angelology and demonology. The archangels were each assigned an area of protection: humans, animals, fire, metal, water, earth, and plants. Lesser angels were given other duties, including one angel being assigned to each day of the year. Demons, likewise, had their duties, which included promoting evils, such as disease, perversity, and greed, but also less harmful jobs, such as teaching or guarding treasures. This led to a complex system of correspondences that influenced magic rituals. Zoroastrianism influenced the angelologies and demonologies of Judaism and Christianity as well as the magical practice of summoning angels and demons.

EMANATIONS

There are two areas in which the Babylonians have contributed religious or philosophical ideas that became the foundation for important occult theories. The first is the concept of **emanation**. Emanation is the belief that the creation of the world took place in stages, or emanations, that flow out of one another or give birth to one another instead of happening all at once. The Babylonians were not the only people to think this way; it is common to many early polytheistic religions. The Babylonians, however, were the ones who influenced the philosophers who later influenced the occultists.

The Babylonian creation story is called the *Enuma Elish.* It took the form of an epic poem that would be recited aloud every year at

The Wise King Solomon

According to legend, one of the greatest magicians of all time was Solomon, the great Old Testament king of Israel, who ruled a united Israel during the golden age in the tenth century B.C.E. and built the First Temple of Jerusalem. In the Bible Solomon is noted for his wisdom but in the Islamic Koran he is also noted for his magical powers. The Koran says Solomon ruled people and spirits alike, and that demons and **genies** did his bidding, including bringing him great wealth and helping in the construction of the temple.

In the Rabbinical literature it is said that his power over demons came from his magical signet ring called "the Seal of Solomon." In one famous tale from *One Thousand and One Nights,* a genie displeased Solomon and he used his ring to seal him in a brass bottle and threw it into the sea where a sailor found it centuries later. It is believed that the signet or Seal of Solomon on his ring was a six-pointed star enclosed in a circle, a design that is familiar today as the symbol of Judaism.

the great ziggurat in Babylon as part of the New Year's celebration. The *Enuma Elish* recounts how the world was created in seven days by the Babylonian gods. It also recounts how the world evolved into its present state through a process of seven emanations as the gods gave birth to one another. In the beginning the goddess Tiamat, whose name means salt water, and her consort Apsu, whose name means fresh water, emerged from the primal waters to become the mother and father of all life. Tiamat was a dragon-like primitive creature, more demon than goddess. She represented the messy chaotic state that existed before the gods imposed order and harmony on the world. She gave birth to Lahmu and Lahamu, whose names both mean silt. From Lahamu emerged Kishar, sea, and her consort, Ansher, sky. In turn, Kishar gave birth to the god Anu, heavens and power, and he with an unnamed mate gave birth to Ea, earth and intellect. Ea killed his great-great grandfather, Apsu, and then mated with Damkina to father the hero Marduk and a host of other gods, who became Marduk's subjects. The newcomers, who represented order and intelligence, caused trouble for the older gods, who represented primitive chaos. A struggle for domination began in which Tiamat with her new consort, Kingu, gave birth to a hoard of monsters to destroy the younger gods.

This battle ended when Marduk killed Tiamat. He split her corpse in two and from the halves created the two parts of the world, heaven and earth. As a result, Marduk was made the king of the gods, like Zeus in classical mythology. Later Marduk slew Tiamat's oafish consort, Kingu, took some of Kingu's divine blood, and mixed it with dust to create the last emanation, humans, who were born to serve the gods. On the seventh day of the *Enuma Elish*, the gods rejoiced in the center of the world, at what is now Babylon, and built the great ziggurat as a temple to Marduk. From the summit of the ziggurat, Marduk put the world in order and gave the gods their duties.

Many details in the *Enuma Elish* are identical to the Bible's account of the creation, which also took place in seven days. Many scholars agree that the Bible story is based on the older Babylonian myth. The

Figure 2.2 *The Babylonian hero-god Marduk raises his weapons in battle.* (Ernest Lehner, *Symbols, Signs, and Signets* [1950])

Hebrew authors identified Marduk with their god, Jehovah, and had him create the world and bring order out of chaos but, being monotheistic, they had no place in their theology for the other gods. In the

Bible, therefore, the concept of emanation was left out. The menorah in the ancient Temple of Jerusalem was said to symbolize the burning bush but its seven oil lamps also symbolized the seven days of creation.

SEVEN WANDERERS

The number seven is considered one of the most magical numbers. It plays an important part in the creation in the *Enuma Elish* and in the Bible. It is because of these creation stories that there are seven days in the week and the world is still said to have seven continents and seven seas. How this number came to be so important has to do with the sky. The Babylonians and their predecessors spent a lot of time observing the sky for messages from the gods, called omens. This practice led to the development of astrology and the discovery of the seven planets.

There are actually eight planets in the solar system. (There used to be nine, but Pluto was reclassified as a dwarf planet along with Eris and three others.) To all ancient peoples, however, there were seven planets. The Sun and the Moon were included in the list but the Earth was not. This was because from Earth, the objects in the sky appear to circle Earth, and she seems to be standing still.

The stars in the night sky have their positions fixed in relation to each other. Groups of stars that form patterns that suggest familiar shapes or images are called constellations. The constellations move as a unit through the sky, except for the ones circling the North Star, they rise in the east and set in the west. Against this canopy of fixed lights there are other, brighter celestial bodies that move at a pace independent from the background. Some of these wanderers even occasionally move west to east against the current. The path they follow is called the ecliptic, and the circle of 12 constellations that this path cuts through is called the zodiac. With the naked eye, seven bright wanderers are visible. In Greek they were called *planetes*, which means "wanderers," and is the origin of the English word planet. To the ancient Babylonians and the people whom they influenced, such as

Figure 2.3 *A Roman triumphal arch panel shows the temple menorah among the spoils of the Second Temple of Jerusalem.* (Wikimedia Commons)

the Greeks, there were seven planets that circled Earth: the Sun, the Moon, Mercury, Venus, Mars, Jupiter, and Saturn.

Ancient peoples considered these seven, brighter, untouchable celestial bodies to be governors of Earth. The Babylonians considered them gods. Astrology is based on the idea that the soul departs from heaven, which is above the stars, through one of the constellations of the zodiac and then descends through the planets to live in a body on planet Earth. At each planet the god of that sphere clothes the soul in certain qualities that become its personality. The astrological natal chart is an attempt to map that process. Effectively, the planets functioned as a ladder or stairway to Earth and as personal emanations or steps in every person's individual creation. Through a complex system of correspondences between the planets and colors, metals, herbs, and other objects on Earth, magicians could use the powers of the planetary gods in their magical practice.

One of the most impressive magical objects to do this was the great ziggurat at Babylon. This was considered a temple to Marduk and called the **Etemenanki**, which means "the gateway to heaven." The Etemenanki no longer exists. It was in ruins by the time ancient Greek visitors wrote about it. From ancient accounts and from studies of other pyramids it is believed to have been a step pyramid made of brick, with about a 300-foot-wide square base, which was aligned with the four cardinal directions. It had seven steps, or levels, reaching 300 feet high and each step had an outer coating of glazed or painted bricks of a different color.

The Etemenanki was said to have been created by the gods and was central to the events told in the *Enuma Elish*. It is likely, therefore, that its seven steps were related to the seven days of creation or the seven emanations of the *Enuma Elish*. Other evidence suggests that the seven steps were also related to the seven gods of the planets and that the color of each step was chosen because of its magical correspondence with each planet. This evidence includes that its name meant the gateway or stairway to heaven, that Nebuchadnezzar called it the Temple of the Seven Lights of the Earth, and that later commentators claimed a connection between its steps and the planets. The Etemenanki then would have become a symbol of the personal astrological ladder of emanations. To climb up it would be a symbolic reversal of the descent into the world of matter: an ascent back to the world of spirit. Figure 2.4 is an artist's conception of the Etemenanki with one possible system of correspondences illustrated.

THE GREEKS

In the world of the ancient Greeks, magical religious cults called the Eleusinian Mysteries served the same function as the cult of Osiris and Isis did for the Egyptians. By performing a ritual based on the myth of a god or hero the participants in the mysteries would have a transformative mystical experience that would assure them of life after death. The oldest mystery cult was based on the myth of the hero Orpheus, who used his harp as a magic tool to charm humans, animals, plants, and rocks alike. When Orpheus' wife, Eurydice, died of a snakebite, he went to Hades, the underworld, and attempted to use his magic to bring her back. As in the story of Isis, the search for enlightenment took the form of a lover's search for his or her lost love.

The Greek Mysteries were a major influence on the Western practice of white magic. One of first groups of magicians to be influenced was the mystical school of philosophy founded by Pythagoras (c. 580–c. 500 B.C.E.). Pythagoras was a great mathematician who is credited with the geometric theorem that determined that the square of the hypotenuse (the long side with two sharper angles) of a right triangle is equal in area to the squares of the other two sides added together. He was, however, as interested in the symbolism of numbers as he was in their use in geometry. He also saw a connection between music and numerical order, and this type of reasoning led to sacred geometry. Pythagoras was the first person to call himself a philosopher, which was a title more like sage or mystic at the time. In the ancient world he was spoken of with reverence and awe. It was said that he had a golden thigh, that he could be in two

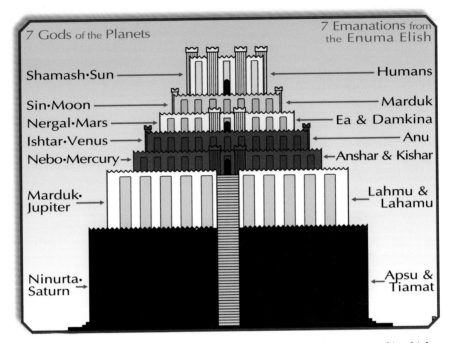

Figure 2.4 *The gods supposedly built the ancient temple Etemenanki, which was dedicated to Marduk. The seven steps on the temple are probably related to the seven days of creation or the seven emanations of the Enuma Elish.* (Robert M. Place)

places at one time, that he could charm animals, and that he could remember his past lives. Many believed he was a god or at least an enlightened master.

THE TETRACTYS

In the Pythagorean school, 10 was considered the perfect number. To represent the numerical intelligence of the universe, the Pythagoreans constructed a triangular arraignment of 10 dots with one at the top, two on the second layer, three on the third, and four at the base. This symbol was called the **Tetractys**, and the Pythagoreans considered it sacred (see Figure 2.5). The Tetractys expressed the concept of emanation in its simplest form, from the greatest unity, the One, to the diversity of the world of form that was associated with four directions, four seasons, and four elements. The most important aspect of this symbol to the mystic was that it could be used as a meditative tool, a ladder, which he or she could use to visualize an ascent back to Oneness. This was a state of being connected to the universe and to the part of an individual that is permanent and beyond the reaches of death.

Many classes of symbolism can be attached to the Tetractys. One of the most basic is a geometrical progression. With this theme the single dot at the top depicts the point, a theoretical beginning with no dimension. The second layer has two points, which describe a line. Although a line has length it has no depth and cannot be perceived any easier than the point. Next, are three points, which are necessary to form the first polygon: the triangle. This provides a two-dimensional plane. The base has four points, which allows the formation of the first three-dimensional object, the tetrahedron, which is composed of four triangular sides, like a pyramid with a triangle for a base. This is the beginning of physical reality.

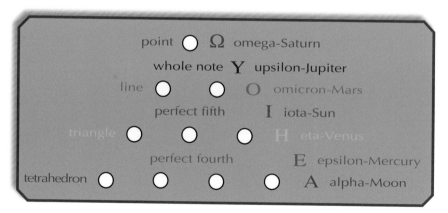

Figure 2.5 *This Pythagorean Tetractys has geometric and musical correlations listed, and the layers are marked with the Greek vowels and their relationships to the seven planets.* (Robert M. Place)

The relationships between the layers are ratios. They describe numerically the vibrations of the three essential notes in the music scale: the whole note, which had a ratio of one to two; the perfect fifth, which has a ratio of two to three; and the perfect fourth, which has a ratio of three to four. Together with the four physical layers, these musical layers provide seven layers altogether. Like the ziggurat the Tetractys had seven layers, but here numbers have replaced the gods as emanations. To fill out the musical scale Pythagoras devised four other notes and created the Western diatonic scale with seven notes. Pythagoras believed that the seven notes captured the sound of each of the seven planets—the music of the spheres—and he used the seven vowels of the Greek alphabet to denote them.

ALEXANDRIA AND THE HERMETIC TRADITION

In the fourth century B.C.E the Macedonian general Alexander the Great (356–323 B.C.E.) defeated the Persian Empire and created a larger one of his own. In 332 B.C.E., shortly after he had added Egypt to his empire, he founded the city of Alexandria near the mouth of the Nile River. After Alexander's death his general, Ptolemy, and his descendants took over the rulership of Egypt. Alexandria became the capital. Because of its position on the delta, Alexandria was a major port and it soon became the largest, most prosperous city in the ancient world. It retained this claim until it became part of the Roman Empire at the death of the last Ptolemaic ruler, Cleopatra VII, in 30 B.C.E. After this it lost its position as the largest city to Rome but it was still the world center of commerce and learning.

Besides its Egyptian inhabitants, Alexandria had a large population of Greeks and the world's largest population of Jews. Greek language and learning were the elements that united these populations, but in Alexandria, Egyptian and Jewish culture merged with Greek to become one Hellenistic culture. In this cultural melting pot the mystical Egyptian god Thoth, the god of magic and words of power, was amalgamated with the Greek Hermes, the god of communication, magic, and wisdom. In the Egyptian texts the name, Thoth, was customarily followed by a triple title, such as the great, great, greatest god. In Greek, Thoth's name was translated as

Western Mystical Traditions

Alchemy: This ancient science synthesized Hermetic mysticism with chemical experimentation. Its main objective was the creation of the magical transformative substance called the Philosopher's Stone. Alchemy is the precursor of modern physics, chemistry, and medicine.

Gnosticism: This is a modern classification for groups of ancient mystics who sought a higher state of consciousness, which they termed *gnosis*, a Greek word for knowledge. These groups include Hermeticists and Jewish Essenes but the term is primarily used to refer to early Christian seekers. Christian Gnosticism maintains a negative view of the physical world and attempts to free the soul from the prison of the body and its physical restraints.

Hermeticism: This is the philosophy followed by a group of Hellenistic mystics and their heirs who sought enlightenment or gnosis through the teachings of the mythical sage Hermes Trismegistus. Many of the Hermetic texts were focused on alchemy and astrology.

Kabalah: This Jewish mystical tradition emerged in the twelfth century in Spain but was based on earlier teachings, such as those described in the second to seventh century Sepher Yetzirah, which merged Neoplatonic concepts with Jewish tradition. The Kabalah influenced the Christian mystic Ramon Llull (1236–1315), and in the late fifteenth century a Christian version of the Kabalah was founded by the Neoplationist Pico della Mirandola (1463–1494).

Hermes but, to show that the Egyptian Hermes was being referred to, the title Trismegistus, meaning thrice great, was added to form Hermes Trismegistus.

Mystical Christianity: This term describes various Christian ascetic traditions that sought a personal vision of God and made use of Neo-platonic ideas. Mystical Christianity has been part of the religion from its beginning in the first century. Notable Christian mystics are Ramon Llull (1236–1315), St. Francis of Assisi (1181 or 1182–1226), Meister Eckhart (c.1260–c.1328), and Teresa of Avila (1515–1582).

Neoplatonism: This group of Western mystical philosophies emerged in the first centuries after Christ and synthesized Platonic philosophy with Hermeticism and other mystical philosophies. It also revived interest in the Pythagorean school. The first Neoplationists were the Hellenistic philosopher Plotinus (204–70) and his teacher Ammonius Saccas (third century).

Occultism: Occult means "hidden," and occultism refers to the study of hidden wisdom, which comes from an inner spiritual study. This is in contrast to science, which studies observable, measurable phenomena. The term is most often applied to the initiates of secret magical societies that began to emerge in Western Europe in the seventeenth and eighteenth centuries, such as the Rosicrucians and the Freemasons.

Sufism: This Islamic mystical tradition has been part of the religion from its beginning in the seventh century. The ascetic Hasan al Basri (642–728 or 737) is considered the first to inspire this teaching. Sufis merged Neo-platonic and Hermetic ideas with Islamic teachings. They were influential in medieval Spain. They inspired the Spanish Christian mystic Ramon Llull and helped to revive Neoplatonism in Western Europe.

The mystic followers of Hermes Trismegistus, known as Hermeticists, believed that Hermes was the true source of their wisdom. When they wrote, they felt that it was a magical act and that the words came from their god; they believed they were channeling Hermes. Some may have even believed that they were re-creating the ancient *Book of Thoth*. In recognition of this fact, they signed their written works with his name instead of their own. These works became known as the Hermetic texts and included works on alchemy, magic, astrology, and philosophy. The philosophic texts were gathered in a collection of 20 texts and collectively called the ***Hermetica***.

Although it was written in the first centuries after the birth of Christ, the *Hermetica* presented itself as an older work written by an ancient sage, named Hermes, who through mystical practices attained a state of higher consciousness and became a god. In the *Hermetica* the word ***gnosis***, a Greek word meaning "knowledge," was used to describe the state of higher consciousness. This same word was used by other mystical seekers at that time, including early Christian sects, known as Gnostics, and some Jewish sects, such as the Essenes. Through the attainment of gnosis, the Hermeticists believed that they too could join the ranks of the immortals, which is the highest goal of magic. They believed that the *Hermetica* was a textbook that taught this procedure, a guidebook to gnosis.

To guide its readers the *Hermetica* used the mystical astrological worldview discussed in this chapter. It described how humans are at heart spiritual beings, who have descended through the ladder of the seven planets into the world of matter, received a body, and lost their way. To find their way back, the *Hermetica* instructs one to visualize in a trance or meditative state that one is ascending back up the ladder of the planets and letting go of the body and all worldly concerns and distractions. This practice leads to gnosis and the realization that one is made of spirit and light.

SEVEN HERMETIC CONCEPTS

Hermetic philosophy became a major influence on all Western magical practices and mystical traditions. **Neoplatonism**, alchemy, Gnosticism, **Kabalah**, **Sufism**, mystical Christianity, and occultism are included in this influence. There are seven basic concepts that make up this view.

1   **The world is a living being:** To the Hermeticists, all of the world, including rocks and streams, is alive and possesses a soul. The physical world was believed to be made of four physical elements: earth, air, fire, and water. The elements would scatter, however, and the entire world would fall apart if they were not held together by the mysterious fifth element, the world soul, or Anima Mundi. This is in contrast with the modern scientific, materialist philosophy, which views the world as composed of nonliving matter.

2   **The mind and physical reality are connected:** Modern science is based on the assumption that there is no connection between the mind and physical reality. To the Hermeticist it is evident that they are connected. The mind, therefore, can cause physical changes and physical objects, such as talismans, can change the mind.

3   **The value of imagination:** In scientific reasoning, the imagination may be useful for inspiration but once an experiment has begun it is considered a contaminant to be weeded out. It takes one out of reality. To the Hermeticist, the imagination is real. It is the door for entering the reality of the soul. Without imagination the soul is not perceptible. The skill at focusing the imagination is gained through the practice of meditation.

4   **The idea of correspondence:** This is the Hermetic view that there is more than a symbolic connection between celestial and terrestrial objects or the Macrocosm and Microcosm. This is often stated as, "as

above, so below." To the Hermeticist the planets are gods or angels and they are also alive in animals, minerals, and plants as well as in the heavens. The magician can use correspondences to harness the celestial powers in his or her ritual. For example, by including iron or red objects in his or her ritual and conducting it on Thursday, the magician can bring the energy of the god Mars to the action.

5 **The belief in transmutation:** To the Hermeticist the world is alive and the goal of all life is to grow and change to become a new and better being. Lead can be turned into gold and a common man into a sage. Ultimately, the goal of life and the greatest good is gnosis, or enlightenment, a mystical transformation that awakes one to the truth of spiritual oneness. The emanations are a spiritual ladder composed of stages or rungs that a magician can make use of to ascend to this goal.

6 **The Perennial Philosophy:** This is the belief that all cultures and religions share common traits or patterns. In its simplest form, it is the belief that all cultures stem from one culture which existed in an ancient golden age or that culture was taught to humans by the gods. In its most sophisticated form, it is the Jungian observation of archetypal patterns in all cultures.

7 **Spiritual truth is gained through transmission or initiation:** This idea stems from the ancient mystery tradition in which one received gnosis by undergoing a ritual initiation. As the initiates in the mysteries were sworn to secrecy, the idea that magical truths must only be shared with others on the same path is also part of this idea.

Magic progressed in the Middle Ages, and during the Renaissance Hermeticism was revived and merged with the Jewish mystical teaching known as Kabalah.

The Practice of Magic

It was the 1580s in England. John Dee was an astronomer, an astrologer, a mathematician, an occultist, a geographer, an alchemist, and an advisor to Queen Elizabeth I. Some claimed that he was her personal magician, a real life Merlin. What many did not know is that he also worked as the Queen's spy, using the code name 007 to sign his letters. This later influenced Ian Fleming, the twentieth century author of the James Bond novels, to assign the same code to his spy hero.

John was one of the most knowledgeable men in England and he had amassed the country's largest library, but when it came to magic he felt that he needed help. He made friends with Edward Kelley, a psychic, who used a crystal ball to contact angels and help John to gather information from the spiritual world. This included learning what he called their Enochian language, a name derived from the biblical descendant of Adam, Enoch, who was said to have visited heaven while alive and talked with angels.

One night, however, the two men were standing in a cemetery at midnight in the center of an intricately drawn **magic circle** designed for a necromantic ritual. John had on his clean black robe and was holding his three-foot wand. Kelley held a torch overhead so that John could read the elaborate invocation. As the ghost was summoned she stood before them outside of the protective circle. Her dress was white and transparent, as was her body, and she had only a skull for a face.

THE MIDDLE AGES

In spite of the fact that magical practices were incorporated into Christian ritual and belief, early Christian theologians began to define magic as heretical and separate from religion. As the Catholic Church came to dominate Western culture in the Middle Ages, this view became the accepted norm. The practice of magic, however, did not stop.

Even before Christianity, people in the classical world feared the negative effects of magic and often blamed their troubles on evil sorcerers or witches. Under Roman law black magic was outlawed but white magic was tolerated and this practice continued under Constantine (272–337), the first Christian to rule the Roman Empire, and his successors. In 438, however, the code became stricter and all forms of magic and divination warranted the death penalty. This swing back and forth in attitude and the law continued through the Middle Ages. As a result, ceremonial magicians became more secretive but folk magic continued to be practiced without much notice.

The Middle Ages is often portrayed in popular fiction as a time when witch hunters were busy burning women for practicing folk magic or for healing their neighbors with herbs. But the church was not concerned with witchcraft during most of the Middle Ages. In fact, during the time of Charlemagne (747–814), the first Holy Roman emperor, belief in witchcraft was considered to be a pagan superstition and anyone who dared to burn a witch, or stake a vampire for that matter, would be condemned as a heretic and receive the death penalty.[1] Even after witchcraft was listed as a crime in the thirteenth century, witches were only asked to repent. They were not executed.

Actual witch burnings and other executions did not heat up until 1450 and continued until the early 1700s. This period falls firmly in the Renaissance and surprisingly coincides with a revitalization of Hermeticism and the development of modern science. It is doubtful that the witch trials had much to do with magic, and they were not entirely focused on women. The evidence from trials shows that midwives or herbalists were rarely accused and in some places a man was more likely to be condemned than a woman. Besides this, the details of the accusations and the forced confessions, which include flying away to meet the devil at a Sabbath where witches committed obscene acts and ate babies, is not believable. Throughout history these same types of wild accusations were directed toward unpopular religious groups or political rivals. The ancient Romans accused Christians of performing obscene rituals where they ate babies, and medieval Christians often made this same claim about Jews.[2]

KABALAH

One of the most important developments in occult tradition to occur in the Middle Ages was the Jewish magical practice called Kabalah. The name Kabalah means "received or oral tradition" in Hebrew. It can be transliterated as Kabala, Kabalah, Kabbala, or the same three combinations beginning with the letter *Q* or the letter *C* instead of a *K*. Kabalah is a mystical or magical Jewish tradition that developed in Spain and southern France in the twelfth century. At that time two influential books were written explaining its philosophy and principles: the *Sepher La-Bahir*, the Book of Brilliance, and the *Sepher ha-Zohar*, the Book of Splendor.

Like the *Hermetica*, these works claimed an older authorship to give their message a more ancient heritage. The Kabalah does, however, stem from an older, oral heritage, and its theories are built on the foundation presented in the *Sepher Yetzirah*, the Book of Creation. This was written between the second and the seventh centuries c.e. in Palestine at a time after the Temple of Jerusalem was destroyed, and Jews were forced to redefine their religion. It seems that they incorporated certain aspects of Hellenistic and Pythagorean mystical philosophy and synthesized this with their biblical heritage and the sacred texts that were written outside of the Bible, called the *Apocrypha*.

Many apocryphal texts were concerned with protection from demons, but others helped to create a Jewish path to gnosis. Some of these texts in the *Apocrypha* were inspired by the story of Enoch, a descendant of Adam who, according to the Bible, ascended to heaven while he was still alive. Because of this feat, Enoch became a model and guide for Jewish mystics, who while in a trance, attempted to ascend the ladder of the seven planets and enter heaven. In heaven they found a similar layered structure leading up to the throne of God in Seventh Heaven. As this is similar to the Hermetic meditation on the seven planets and as Hermes was the model and guide for that ascent, it was natural that Enoch was equated with Hermes Trismegistus. The names Enoch, Thoth, and Hermes became synonymous in the texts of the Kabalah.

In the *Sepher Yetzirah*, which claims Abraham, the founder of Judaism, as its author, the image of the Tree of Life, which grew in the center of Eden, and the Hermetic ladder of the planets were combined into one diagram which was said to be the vehicle of God's creation. The diagram consists of 10 energized centers or circles, called **sephiroth**, arranged in a vertical pattern. The sephiroth served as emanations in the creation of the world. As in the Hermetic practice, a mystic was invited to climb them in meditation.

In Hebrew each letter also serves as a number, and the letters in words can be added to find their numerical value. In the kabalistic practice called **gematria**, these numeric values have meaning, and words with similar numeric value are said to be connected.

In the twelfth century Jewish mystics used gematria in their meditations to find the secret names of God. They hoped to use these empowered names in their magical assent to heaven and to attain gnosis. Ten names or qualities of God were discovered and these were assigned to the 10 sephiroth on the Tree of Life. These qualities can be translated into English as:

1 Crown

2 Wisdom

3 Intelligence

4   Greatness

5   Power

6   Beauty

7   Endurance

8   Majesty

9   Foundation

10 Kingdom

Also, 22 pathways were created between the sephiroth, and each was assigned one of the 22 Hebrew letters. As one meditated on each letter in this system, one progressed up the tree of life and moved toward the mystical goal.

THE CHRISTIAN KABALAH

One of the first Christians to become interested in the Kabalah was the Spanish nobleman Ramon Llull (1236–1315). Growing up in Majorca, Ramon came to admire the mystical teaching of the Islamic Sufis and the Jewish kabalists, but he longed to create a Christian version of these teachings. He developed his own system called the **Ars Magna**, for which he created emanations based on the qualities of God like the sephiroth on the Tree of Life. In Llull's system he had nine emanations instead of 10 because nine is three times three—the number of the Trinity. His emanations were:

1   Goodness

2   Greatness

3   Purity

4   Power

5   Wisdom

6   Free will

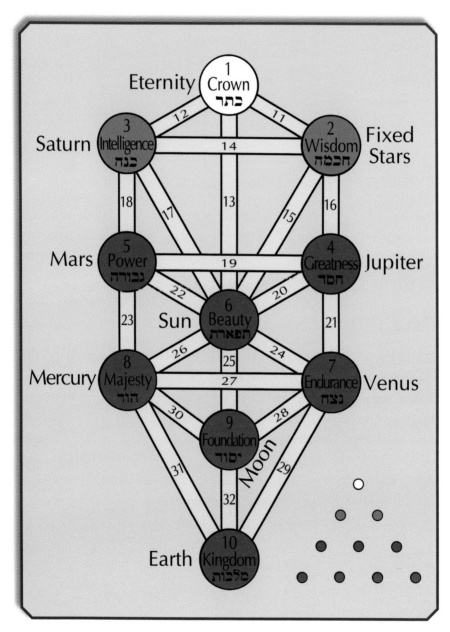

Figure 3.1 *The sephiroth on the kabalistic Tree of Life are colored to show their connection to the dots on the Tetractys, depicted on the lower right. The planetary correlations are listed beside each sephiroth.* (Robert M. Place)

7 Strength

8 Truth

9 Glory

Each was assigned an initial and, through a complex system of correspondences, associated with all arts, sciences, and natural objects. It is interesting to note that Llull was also the first author of a medieval romance, the genre of literature that led to the tales of King Arthur, Merlin the magician, and the mystical quest for the Holy Grail.

During the Renaissance, Christian interest in the Kabalah was revived by the Neoplatonist Pico della Mirandola (1463–1494). Pico was friends with the famous Renaissance Neoplatonist Marsilio Ficino (1433–1499), who translated the works of Plato into Latin. In 1460 Ficino received a Greek text of the *Hermetica*, and he stopped work on Plato to translate the entire text into Latin for the first time. Pico studied the Kabalah with a friend who had converted from Judaism to Christianity and published kabalistic texts translated into Latin. Pico believed that the Kabalah contained a lost divine revelation. This was a mystical key that underlaid the teachings of the Orphics, Pythagoras, and Plato, and demonstrated that all ancient mystical philosophy culminated in the teachings of Christ. Pico synthesized the Kabalah with Hermeticism and Christianity and presented it to the intellectuals of the Renaissance. His influence spread to Germany where Johannes Reuchlin (1455–1522) published two books on the Kabalah in the early sixteenth century. The Holy Roman Emperor Maximilian (1456–1519) drew Kabalists to his court in Germany. It was there that the famous magician Heinrich Cornelius Agrippa (1486–1535), who was in the emperor's service as a knight for a brief time, wrote his *Occult Philosophy*, first published in 1531. In *Occult Philosophy*, Agrippa made use of kabalistic divine names in his magic invocations and synthesized the Kabalah with Hermeticism and Neoplationism. After this, the name Kabalah was synonymous with magic and alchemy.

Figure 3.2 *Ramon Llull's diagram of his Ars Magna includes the nine emanations written in a circle in Latin and the initial assigned to each in the outer circle.* (Ramon Llull)

Besides being used for finding the secret names of God, the kabalistic practice of gematria was helpful for finding the names of angels and demons. Ceremonial magicians craved this knowledge. In the late Middle Ages and Renaissance, kabalistic names and techniques appeared in magician's how-to books, called **grimoires**.

GRIMOIRES

Grimoires are magical textbooks that began to appear in the late Middle Ages. As magicians never knew if they would be persecuted for their practice, they tended to keep these books secret. As a result it is hard to determine when they first appeared. The oldest ones seem to be based on kabalistic grimoires, such as *Sefer Raziel HaMalakh*, the Book of the Angel Raziel, written in Hebrew and Aramaic in the thirteenth century. These kabalistic texts in turn were influenced by the Greek Magical Papyri, a group of Hellenistic Egyptian texts written from the second century B.C.E. to the fifth century C.E.

The most popular medieval grimoire was *The Key of Solomon*, which gave instructions for raising spirits, angels, or demons. Another

An Ancient Demon

Some of the angels and demons summoned by magicians in the Renaissance had ancient roots. The Zoroastrians gave the name Aeshma Daeva to the sixth archdemon under Ahriman, the prince of darkness, and made him the sprit of decay and fury. In Hebrew demonology he was known as Ashmadai. The Christians called him Asmodeus, and that is the name used in the grimoires of the Renaissance.

As depicted, he was said to have three heads, one human and the others of a bull and a ram. He also has the feet of a goose and a snake for a tail. In some depictions, he appears to be riding another beast. The grimoires, however, say that he is not to be feared. If one addresses him properly he will provide a beautiful ring, and then teach geometry, arithmetic, astronomy, and engineering, as well as the art of being invisible, and the location of hidden treasure.[3]

grimoire, *The Sacred Magic of Abra-Melin the Sage*, became popular later and was used extensively by magicians even into the twentieth century. The grimoires provided the most complete description of magical preparation and practice since the ancient Egyptian texts. Here is a list of the types of instructions often found in a grimoire:

- **Purpose of the ritual**: Ceremonial magic can be used to accomplish many things; cursing or destroying an enemy or rival; attracting wealth or a lover; or the ultimate goal, increasing one's power in an effort to become like a god. Of course in the highest form of magic the ultimate goal is to become enlightened. To accomplish the goal the magician will enlist spiritual aid by summoning a spirit, an angel, a demon, or a god. A magician may also summon the spirit of a person who has died. This is called **necromancy**. It is often classed as a type of divination because the dead were said to have knowledge of the future, and this knowledge was what the necromancer sought.

- **Preparation of the magician:** Preparation includes the training of the mind through meditation and prayer, but it also includes purification. Besides praying and focusing the mind on the object of the ritual for weeks before beginning, the magician is often instructed to abstain from sex and food for this period and to maintain strict cleanliness. A magician soiled in his or her mind or body is inviting demonic invasion.

- **Choosing a place**: The best place for a magic ritual is one where spirits reside, such as a graveyard, a church, or a deserted crossroad, but a magician may prefer his or her own dwelling, which has been magically charged through meditative practice.

- **Choosing a time**: The best time is usually at night when spirits are more active. The magician may also use astrology to determine the best day and hour to assure the success of the ritual.

- **Preparing the place**: The most important aspect of preparation is the drawing of a magic circle that the magician will stand in.

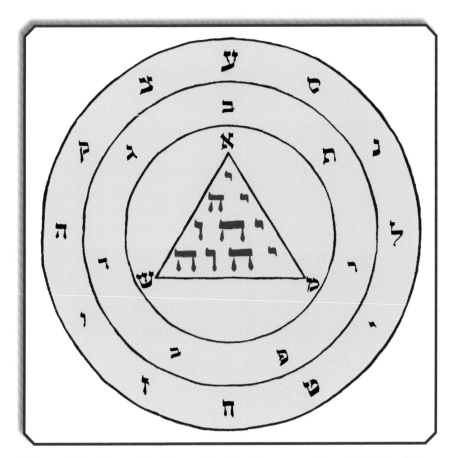

Figure 3.3 *This magic circle contains the Tetragrammaton with the four letters arranged as a Tetractys in green in the central triangle. The three letters outside of the corners of the triangle represents the elements air, water, and fire. The seven letters in the next circle represent the seven planets. The 12 letters in the outer circle represent the 12 signs of the Zodiac.* (Sefer Yetzirah [Sixth-century copy])

Although it is circular, this is more of a **mandala** filled with symbols, magic names, and inscriptions than a simple circle. It is drawn on the floor or the ground and meant to protect the magician during the ritual. One of the most common protections to be included on the rim is the four-letter name of God in Hebrew, known as the **Tetragrammaton**, usually transliterated as Yahweh or Jehovah. If a magician made an error when drawing the circle or neglected to stay inside during the ritual, it is said that this mistake could prove fatal.

○ **The proper tools and dress**: The magician most often wore a clean white robe for the ritual, but other colors, such as black may be appropriate for certain purposes. Like all ritual tools, the robe should be new and clean. The magician's tools include candles, incense, herbs, and oils that are chosen to harmonize with the spirit being summoned or to stimulate the magician's psychic abilities. Other tools can include a magic wand, a sword, a chalice, and various talismans in the form of **magic squares** or circular designs often referred to as **pentacles or pentagrams**. This example of a magic square, seen below, is from *The Sacred Magic of Abra-Merlin the Sage*, designed to allow a magician to fly in the form of a crow.

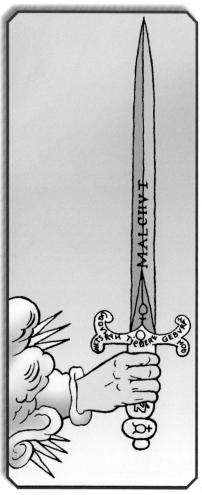

Figure 3.4 *Magicians commonly use swords as tools while performing rituals.* (Eliphas Levi, *The Magical Ritual of the Sanctum Regnum* [1896])

```
R O L O R
O B U F O
L U A U L
O F U B O
R O L O R
```

○ **The proper incantation:** Essentially, the incantation is a form of words of power and this is the main part of the ritual. As with

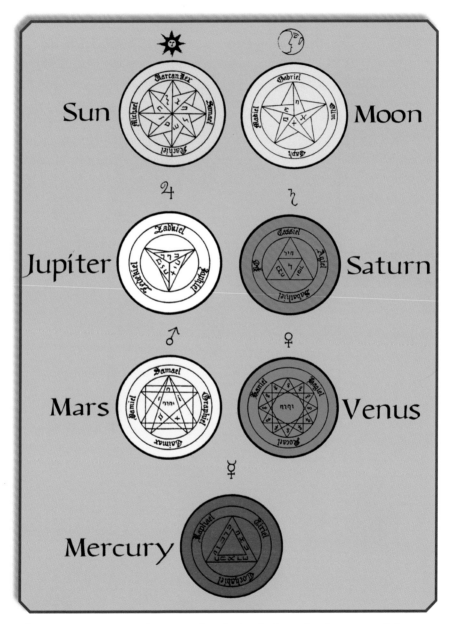

Figure 3.5 *Pentacles from a medieval grimoire bear the the names of the angels associated with each of the seven planets.* (Manly P. Hall, *The Secret Teachings of All Ages* [1995])

the circle, the incantation must be said correctly or bad things can happen. An important part of the incantation is knowledge of the name of the spirit being summoned. Magicians believe that there is a magical connection between any being and its name. When properly pronounced a spirit cannot resist being summoned by name.

The magical synthesis that was created in the sixteenth century included Kabalah, Hermeticism, magic, and alchemy. The next chapter looks at what alchemists were doing during the centuries that led up to this period.

The History of Alchemy

It was the middle of the fourteenth century in Italy, and once again Ernesto was working in his laboratory late at night. For many years he dreamed of discovering the elusive Philosopher's Stone. He had spent most of his inheritance in this effort; buying expensive books filled with puzzling illustrations and instructions written in code; supplying his laboratory with glass vessels and a furnace; and buying expensive metals, especially the gold he needed to seed the substance growing in his glass retort. He had also had many false starts over the years in which all of his expenses and his work had achieved nothing. This time, however, he believed that all of his efforts had finally paid off. As he stood looking at his work, slowly heating in the furnace, a glow began to form in the vessel that grew brighter and brighter until the light filled the room. This was the sign he was looking for.

THE HISTORY OF ALCHEMY

Alchemy is as confusing a subject as magic. If asked to give a meaning for the word, ancient alchemists would have given as many definitions as there were alchemists. One thing that they could all agree on, however, was that the central purpose of alchemy is transmutation. Transmutation is an event in which one substance is changed into another. Alchemists believed that transmutation was possible and made it the main focus of their work. The most famous

Figure 4.1 *An alchemist in his laboratory looks at the glow forming in his glass retort.* (Joseph Wright, *The Alchemist in Search of the Philosopher's Stone Discovers Phosphorus* [circa 1771–1775])

example is their belief that they could change lead, an inexpensive metal, into gold, one of the most valuable. Although some alchemists treated it that way, alchemy was not simply a get-rich-quick scheme.

Alchemists also believed that they could transform themselves into an enlightened sage.

Alchemists hoped to accomplish transmutation through the interaction of a magical catalyst called the Philosopher's Stone. The creation of the Philosopher's Stone, therefore, became the central purpose or the Great Work of all alchemists. The Philosopher's Stone was said to be a mystical substance: a stone that is not a stone. It could cure any illness, prolong life indefinitely, and transform any metal into its highest state. It is not clear if the stone could also transform the alchemist to his or her highest state or if it was the Great Work itself that accomplished this, but this was also the goal. Some alchemical texts focus on creating the stone through lab work, and these were the precursors of modern medicine and chemistry. Others, however, focus on alchemy as an internal mystical process that takes place in the mind of the alchemist.

EGYPTIAN ORIGIN

Although separate alchemical traditions exist in India and China, Western alchemy emerged out of Egypt. Initially, it dealt with metals and although connected with magic it was not viewed as a spiritual path. Egyptian religion evolved out of a shamanistic prehistoric past, and in this process developed a complex body of magic formulas that were the beginning of what would later be called geology, metallurgy, and chemistry. Among these were the techniques for separating metals from ore, the making of such alloys as bronze by combining copper and tin, dyeing, brewing, gilding, perfume-making, devising chemical recipes, and reciting magic rituals for the embalming of the dead. Embalming rituals, in particular, are alchemical in nature and seem to be the origin of the Great Work. The body was dismembered, reassembled, then chemically preserved and wrapped. It was placed in a coffin, which is like the alchemical vessel, and was acted on by magic rituals designed to aid the resurrection of the deceased.

Alchemical theories also stem from the ancient Greeks. The Pythagorean philosopher Empedocles (490–430 B.C.E.) developed the theory of the four elements and of the governing principles of attraction and repulsion or love and hate. Later Plato added the four qualities to this theory and assigned two to each element: earth was cold and dry; fire was hot and dry; air was hot and moist; water was cold and moist. Now each of the four elements had a shared quality that allowed the elements to transform into one another.

In the Hellenistic period in Alexandria, starting in 332 B.C.E., Greek culture and philosophy came into contact with Egyptian mystical religion and magic. One could say that this mixture was the beginning of what we know as alchemy in the West. The earliest extant alchemical manuscripts are Egyptian papyruses from Alexandria. They are texts on metallurgy, especially for making imitation metals for jewelry. These recipes call for adding small amounts of gold to other metals to make a product that appears to be all gold. It was the Hermetic texts, however, that gave alchemy its spiritual focus. The basic principles of Hermeticism listed in Chapter 2 apply equally to alchemy.

Modern scholars regard Zosimos, a Greek who lived in Panopolis, Egypt, in the third century C.E. at the end of the Hellenistic period, as the oldest known "authentic" alchemist. His works are known from an encyclopedia-like compendium of 28 alchemical texts, collected in the seventh and eighth centuries in Byzantium. His writing describes the ennobling of base metals into gold by first "killing" them and then "resurrecting" them, a process obviously similar to Egyptian embalming and related to the myth of Osiris.

Alchemists believed that all metals were of one substance but in various states of purity, with gold being the most pure and lead the least. The transformation of lead to gold was considered a natural process that happened in the ground, but it could take centuries to accomplish. The alchemist, with the aid of a catalyst, could produce the change more quickly than nature. Zosimos' method of creating the catalyst depended on a process that took place in four stages determined by color: black, white, yellow, and red, which are obtained through a substance he called the material's sulfur water. To the early alchemists color was the most important characteristic of metal. Thus,

Figure 4.2   *This ouroboros, an important alchemical symbol for time and regeneration, comes from a third-century text attributed to Cleopatra.*   (Robert M. Place)

it was natural that they would look for color changes to mark the stages of their work.

Zosimos named the magical catalyst that was necessary for the transformation of metals "the powder," which was translated into Arabic as *aliksir*, then into Latin as *elixir*, and finally became known as the Philosopher's Stone. Zosimos credits as the source of his knowledge Maria "The Jewess." She may have been a Syrian alchemist from another and older school, although some scholars believe that she is totally mythical.

Like all alchemists, Zosimos followed his dreams and visions in his search for the basic material of the universe, and he experienced mysterious archetypal images of sacrifice and transformation. He conceived of the idea of the god-man, who fell into cosmic matter, from which he had to be freed by alchemy, a vision that is similar to the one expressed in the *Hermetica*. This mystical element of alchemy combined with the metallurgical recipes made for an exotic combination. Another early alchemical work, the *Codex Marcianus*, contains a translated text that asserts that it was written by Isis to her son Horus. In it she tells him the secret of making gold and silver, a secret she coerced from angels.

ARABIC ALCHEMISTS

The Arabian army, under Amribn al-Ass, conquered Egypt by 642, bringing Arabs into contact for the first time with a large group of working alchemists. By the eighth century the Nestorians, who originated in Byzantium, would form another avenue for alchemical knowledge to enter the Arabic world. In the fifth century they had broken from the Orthodox Church and emigrated east, where they taught Hellenistic philosophy and translated Greek texts, including alchemical ones, into their language, Syriae. By the eighth and ninth centuries, Syriae texts were translated into Arabic. Additionally, during this period the Islamic Empire under the Umayyad rulers spread east to the Indus River, where there was ample opportunity to share influences with Indian alchemists. Wherever they encountered it, Arabs were quick to learn the philosophical science. In fact, all great alchemists from the early medieval period wrote in Arabic.

The eighth century Arabian alchemist, Jabir ibn Hayyan (circa 721–815), known in medieval Europe as Geber, was a member of the mystical Islamic movement known as Sufism. Sufis incorporated many

Figure 4.3   *Zosimos' teacher, Maria, points at a symbol of distillation, the process she is said to have invented.* (Michael Maier, *Symbola Aurea Mensae* [1617])

Hermetic and Neoplatonic tenets into their Islamic asceticism. Like all mystics, they strove for a personal experience of the divine, so it was natural that Jabir would be attracted to alchemy. Jabir developed a theory that became common to all subsequent alchemical texts. He said that all metals seemed to contain a balance of the four qualities; that is, they are cold and dry externally, and hot and moist internally. This was due to the fact that they were formed in the earth by the union of a substance that he called sulphur or "earthy smoke," and another, which he called mercury or "moist vapor." Sulphur and mercury became a masculine and feminine polarity in alchemy.

Jabir also infused a great deal of mystical number symbolism into alchemy. He attached great importance to the numbers 1, 3, 5, and 8, which total 17; for instance, he said that metals have 17 powers. It is most likely that these numbers are derived from Neoplatonic magic squares, which were squares divided into nine equal boxes containing numbers that, whether added diagonally or orthogonally, always equaled the same sum. This was a subject of one of Jabir's many written works.

Mohammed ibn Zakariya al-Razi (865–925), a Persian alchemist, introduced the necessity of accurate weights and measures. He recorded, in Arabic, details of his laboratory apparatus, much of which is still used by modern chemists. Parallel to this technical contribution, Mohammed ibn Umail, the tenth century alchemist known in Latin as Senior, added much to the mystical side in his many writings, the most famous of which is the *Turba Philosophorum, a* convention of philosophers, which describes a debate between Hermes, Socrates, Aristotle, and other philosophers.

WESTERN EUROPEAN ALCHEMISTS

Alchemy did not enter mainstream Europe until the twelfth century. It is believed that the Knights Templar were among the first Westerners to be acquainted with alchemy. During the Crusades, the Knights Templar had adopted the teachings of the Druses, a mystical pagan sect within the Islamic world. In the eleventh and twelfth centuries, the Islamic empire in Spain lost territory to Christian rulers. With the help of Jews, who were able to act as intermediaries between the two cultures, Spain became a cultural melting pot.

Jewish and Islamic scholars were invited to the court of Frederick II in Sicily, and the Knights of St. John opened communication with the East on the island of Rhodes. Due to this influx, Sicily, Spain, and southern France rapidly became multicultural communities. In these areas Jewish and other scholars began to translate Arabic and Greek texts into Latin, which made them available to the rest of Europe. One of the first of these texts was the *Book of the Composition of Alchemy,* translated into Latin by the Englishman Robert of Chester in 1144. By the thirteenth and fourteenth centuries, the art of gold-making was integrated into Western mystical philosophy.

Figure 4.4 *European alchemists believed that Hermes Trismegistus was the first alchemist. Behind Hermes in this engraving a phoenix is reborn from a fire, a symbol of the regenerative power of the Philosopher's Stone.* (Johann Daniel Mylius, *Antidotarium* [1620])

European alchemists traced the origin of their craft to the mythic Hermes Trismegistus, who they believed was the first alchemist. The alchemical process came to be called the Magnum Opus or the Great Work. The Magnum Opus was the search for the elusive, transformative substance contained in all matter. This substance was called by various names, such as the Anima Mundi (world soul), the Quinta Essentia (essential fifth element), the Unus Mundus (world of the one), or the Philosopher's Stone. To find it, alchemists had to determine the correct chemical procedure. This was a lengthy and difficult process of trial and error, with obscure symbolic texts as their only guide. The vivid, symbolic, and allegorical nature of alchemy is due to the fact that alchemists relied on direct dreams, visions, and revelation in their work. Since no two alchemists experienced exactly the same dreams and visions, alchemical texts tend to be vague and even contradictory.

Parallel with the study of alchemy in the West there was an interest in mystical symbolic art that was influenced by Egyptian art and hieroglyphs. In 1422 a Greek book called the *Hieroglyphica*, arrived in Florence and was translated into Latin. Allegedly, the *Hieroglyphica* was a Greek translation of an Egyptian work that explained the meaning of Egyptian hieroglyphics. It was actually an ancient Greek text, not a translation, and only passed on a Greek misconception about hieroglyphs. Because the ancient Greeks were unable to read them, they assumed that hieroglyphs were not an ordinary type of writing but allegorical pictures incorporating many aspects of their subject into one image, and inviting the viewer's interpretation.

The *Hieroglyphica* was translated into Latin, French, German, and Italian, and became known throughout Europe. It was a major influence in developing the Renaissance trend for symbolic engravings called emblems or hieroglyphs. These were created by prominent artists, such as Albrecht Dürer and Leonardo da Vinci, and used to encapsulate various fields of knowledge, especially alchemy.

Immortality

Although the quest for immortality is most often interpreted as another way of expressing the quest for enlightenment, many alchemists took the term literally. They wanted to achieve immortality by not actually dying. This is especially evident in the story of the fourteenth century Parisian alchemist Nicholas Flamel. In 1357 Nicholas bought a rare, old, gilded book, *The Book of Abraham the Jew*, filled with strange illustrations and instructions for the transformation of metals into gold. With the help of his wife, Perrenelle, he began the difficult and lengthy process of carrying out the almost incomprehensible instructions. Although they struggled for 25 years, they were not successful. It was the puzzling symbolic illustrations, gathered in the center of the book and not accompanied by any written explanation, that held the secret of the Magnum Opus, and Nicholas did not understand them. He carefully copied them and showed his copies to anyone who came into his bookshop, but this was of no help. In the end, he took the drawings to Spain. There by luck or grace, he met an old Jewish scholar who helped him decipher their meaning. He came home and with his wife he finally created the Philosopher's Stone.

After their success, the couple used the Philosopher's Stone to tranform lead to gold and with their sudden wealth they endowed 14 hospitals, three chapels, and seven churches in Paris and others in Boulogne. They also helped the poor. In their will they left numerous houses as well as money for the benefit of the homeless. According to legend, having also discovered the secret of immortality, the Flamels only faked their deaths and moved to India with enough gold to last many lifetimes. The couple was reported to have been seen at the Paris Opera in 1761, and there are other accounts of their appearing throughout the centuries, the latest being in the first book of the Harry Potter series.

By the seventeenth century interest in alchemy had peaked, and an unprecedented quantity of enigmatically illustrated alchemical books were published, including the many works of Michael Maier (1568–1622), Jacob Böhme (1575–1624), and even a book with pictures and no written text, the *Mutus Liber* (Silent Book) by Isaac Baulot (1612–?), writing under the name Altus.

Paracelsus (1493–1541), one of the greatest alchemists and the founder of modern medicine, defined alchemy as the transformation of one natural substance into another, one fit for a new use. He created non-herbal medicines, which he considered the main physical goal of alchemy. However, he was equally strong in his belief that the true quest of the alchemist was his own spiritual transformation. The students of Paracelsus tended to split in two directions: those who developed the science of medication, which led to modern medicine and then chemistry; and those who abandoned the laboratory to search for spiritual gold within, a course which led to mystical philosophies like Rosicrucianism, a mystical brotherhood that emerged in the seventeenth century.

The spiritual quest had been part of alchemy since ancient times. After Paracelsus it became more and more the primary objective of alchemy. These alchemists wanted to separate themselves from those who were interested in alchemy only as a means to wealth. Solely materialistic alchemists were called puffers because of their impatient use of the bellows to keep the fire hot and speed up the process.

Besides puffers, con men sought riches and fame through fraudulent claims of a successful transformation of base metal into gold, accomplished by trickery. These charlatans caused alchemy to fall into disrepute. In the eighteenth century, fraud plus the discrediting of alchemy's underlying theories by scientific discoveries caused alchemy to be reduced to a pseudoscience. It received the deathblow from the chemist Antoine Lavoisier (1743–1794) when he discovered that air contained an irreducible component which he labeled *oxygine*.

Lavoisier changed the definition of the term *element* to mean one of these irreducible components instead of the classical four. He went on

Figure 4.5 *Paracelsus holds his sword, which has a crystal pommel, or hilt. The pommel contains the alchemical elixir called Zoth or Azoth.* (Paracelsus, *Astronomica et Astrologica Opuscula* [1567])

to develop modern chemical terminology, which now lists 118 elements on the periodic table. In 1808, the chemist John Dalton (1766–1844) wrote that for each element there is a different unit of matter, called an atom, which is indivisible. Although these men contributed greatly to our body of scientific knowledge, by the end of the nineteenth century scientists would prove that their assumptions about the fundamental nature of reality were also wrong. Also, it is interesting to note that, although it was science that demoted alchemy, Isaac Newton (1643–1727), one of the founders of modern science, took alchemy seriously and spent more of his time studying alchemy than he did the theory of gravity.

The Principles of Alchemy

Franz was an alchemist living in seventeenth century Germany, but he did not have a laboratory, nor vessels, nor a furnace. What he did have was a large collection of books, some of them old and rare and all filled with puzzling texts and enigmatic images. Most of the books were in Latin. Some of his favorites were the *Turba Philosophorum* (Assembly of Philosophers), *The Rosarium Philosophorum* (the Rosary of the Philosophers), and Michael Maier's *Atalanta Fugiens* (Atalanta Fleeing).

To Franz alchemy was a meditative practice. He would sit for hours in his study reading his books, and sometimes he would just sit and contemplate one of the illustrations. On several occasions it was an illustration that seemed to open an inner door in his mind and allowed him to travel to a spiritual dimension. Once there, he was able to hold conversations with ancient alchemists and philosophers and sometimes even with angels.

ALCHEMY BY THE NUMBERS

It is not surprising that the word gibberish originally referred to texts written by the medieval Arabic alchemists Jabir, known in Latin as Geber. Many people find alchemy a daunting and confusing subject, and this impression is not entirely unfounded. Every alchemist explained his or her work in personal terms and symbols that were

Figure 5.1 *A group of philosophers have a discussion about alchemy.* (*Turba Philosophorum* [1572])

derived from unique visions. Descriptions of the alchemical process, therefore, vary considerably from alchemist to alchemist. Often the same symbol has a different meaning from one text to another. For example, a green lion in one text may refer to the ore from which antimony is extracted, in another to vitriol, and in yet another it may symbolize mercury in its raw or poisonous state. On top of this, alchemists used deceptive language in their texts to hide their secrets. Also, alchemists used the same symbolic language in texts that are entirely philosophical or theoretical as they do in ones describing lab work.

Luckily, however, most alchemists agreed on several basic concepts and principal stages of the Great Work. These evolved over the centuries but remained framed by a mystical, mathematical system of number symbolism derived from the school of Pythagoras. Evidence of this structure is in the following quote from an alchemical text called *Rosarium Philosophorum:*

> Make a round circle out of the man and woman, and draw
> out of it a quadrangle, and out of the quadrangle a tri-
> angle, make a round circle, and thou shalt have the Stone
> of the Philosophers.[1]

The basic principles of alchemy are associated with numerical symbolism. The following topics are in numerical order.

ONENESS OR UNITY

Oneness in alchemy is represented by the Materia Prima (the first material), the single, invisible, indestructible substance, from which all things derive and to which all things return. It was also known as the Anima Mundi (the world soul), the Quinta Essentia (the essential fifth element) and the Unus Mundus (the one world). Although it is confusing, alchemists also called the initial substance, or raw material that would be used as the subject of the Great Work, the Materia Prima. In this raw state, however, the Anima Mundi or soul was not yet released. If Materia Prima is used in this way, then the final product of the Great Work may be called Materia Ultima (the final or best material). In its primal state before creation, the Materia

Prima can also be called the Massa Confusa, or Chaos, on which the world of form was imposed.

Ruland's *Lexicon of Alchemy*, published in 1612, lists 134 different definitions for Materia Prima, many of which contradict each other, but the Materia Prima is the most important concept in Alchemy. Essentially, it is the substance that unifies everything. It shows that although to our senses things seem to be separate from one another, the world is actually one united thing and we are connected to it. By connecting that concept to the Anima Mundi, alchemists were agreeing with the first principle of Hermeticism that the entire world, including rocks and minerals, has a soul and is, therefore, alive.

DUALITY

To the alchemists duality is an illusion. It is the division of the Unus Mundus into opposite pairs of polarities, which were considered masculine and feminine. The fact that these masculine and feminine pairs attract each other was considered a divine gift in that this allowed them to recombine and return to unity. The alchemical Great Work, therefore, is a process of transmutation in which opposite polarities are combined, separated, and recombined to attain a state beyond duality.

Alchemists identified numerous symbolic pairs of opposites that need to be combined and transformed in the Great Work. The polarities are always masculine and feminine pairs, such as the Red King and White Queen, Sun and Moon, Gold and Silver, or Sulphur and Mercury. These pairs are listed in masculine and feminine columns in Table 5.1.

THREE ESSENCES

Besides being composed of elements, early alchemists believed that there were two essences or principles found in all matter, which they labeled Sulphur and Mercury. These labels should not be confused with the elements sulfur and mercury, which would be composed of the essences like any other material. When Sulphur and Mercury were combined with earth in various levels of purity and impurity the seven metals were formed. As the first two were thought of as operating in

TABLE 5.1: **Alchemical Dualities**	
Masculine	Feminine
King	Queen
Red	White
Sun	Moon
Gold	Silver
Day	Night
Light	Dark
Lion	Eagle
Fixed	Volatile
Wingless Serpent	Winged Serpent
Sulphur	Mercury
Air & Fire	Earth & Water
Warm & Cold	Dry & Moist
Active	Passive
Dry	Wet
Above	Below

earth, the famous sixteenth century alchemist Paracelsus added Salt, representing earth, to the two and created the theory of the three essences: Salt, Sulphur, and Mercury. These three were thought of as the body, mind, and spirit of any substance.

Again, all substances were thought to have mind and spirit along with a body, just like humans, because all substances were believed to be alive. In both ancient Egyptian and classical philosophy these three aspects of a human were each thought to have a governing soul. The Egyptians called these three parts the Ka, the Ba, and the Akh. In the works of the famous Greek philosopher Plato (428–427 B.C.E.–348–347 B.C.E.) these three parts may be equated to the soul of desire, the soul of will, and the soul of reason. The relationship between these triplicities can be seen in Table 5.2.

THE FOURFOLD WORLD

The alchemists believed that everything in the sublunar world, in other words the Earth, which in their view was in the center of the universe below the orbit of the Moon, was composed of four elements. Ordered from the bottom up and from the densest to the most active,

TABLE 5.2: **Alchemical Triplicities**			
ALCHEMICAL QUALITY	Salt	Sulphur	Mercury
HUMAN QUALITY	Body	Mind	Spirit
EGYPTIAN SOULS	Ka	Ba	Akh
PLATO'S SOULS	Soul of Desire	Soul of Will	Soul of Reason

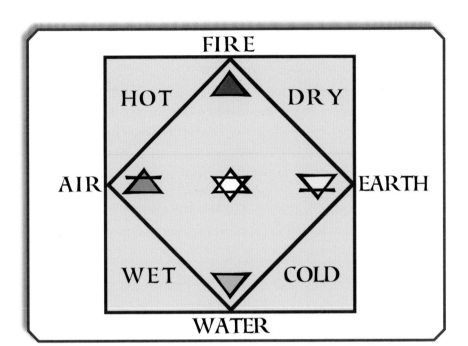

Figure 5.2 *This illustration shows the relationship between the four elements and the four qualities. Alchemical symbols for the elements are shown in the corners of the center diamond. The white star in the center represents the Quinta Essentia, or the fifth element.* (Robert M. Place)

they are: earth, water, air, and fire. The origin of this theory is credited to the ancient Pythagorean philosopher Empedocles (490–430 B.C.E.), who split them into masculine and feminine pairs: earth and water are feminine, and air and fire are masculine.

The fourth century B.C.E. philosopher Plato added four qualities to this theory: hot, dry, wet, and cold: Two of each of these qualities were shared by each element, as can be seen in Figure 5.2, and because of this shared quality one element could transform into another. Alchemists also related the four qualities and elements to four liquid qualities in the body called humors: black bile, phlegm, blood, and yellow bile. They believed that health was attained through the proper balance of these humors. They also believed that an excess of any humor led to four distinct personality types, characterized by sadness, laziness, joy, and anger.

Besides the four elements, the Great Work was divided into four stages and each was characterized by a color: black, white, yellow, and red. The Great Work consisted of separation of the Primary Material into separate masculine and feminine parts that were joined in what was called the lesser conjunction. This substance was subjected to various chemical operations until the substance was killed and left to rot in a process called putrefaction. Next the substance was separated again, bathed and purified, and then recombined in the greater conjunction. This process brought the substance back to life in a spiritual form. Because of the Great Work, the substance

TABLE 5.3: **Alchemical Quadruplicities**				
ELEMENT	**EARTH**	**WATER**	**FIRE**	**AIR**
QUALITIES	Cold & Dry	Cold & Moist	Warm & Dry	Warm & Moist
ALCHEMICAL STAGE	Nigredo	Albedo	Citrinitas	Rubedo
HUMOR	Black Bile	Phlegm	Yellow Bile	Blood
ORGAN	Spleen	Brain & Lungs	Gall Bladder	Liver
SEASON	Winter	Autumn	Summer	Spring
TYPE	Melancholic	Phlegmatic	Choleric	Sanguine
CLASSICAL CHARAC- TERISTICS	Despondent, Sleepless, Irritable	Calm, Unemotional	Easily Angered, Bad Tempered	Courageous, Hopeful, Amorous

had become more spirit and less material until it transforms into the Philosopher's Stone, which is pure spirit.

The first part of the Great Work, up until the putrefaction, is referred to as the Nigredo (the blackening). The second part, in which the substance is separated and purified, is the Albedo (the whitening). The greater conjunction, which is symbolized as a marriage of the moon with yellow sun, is called the Citrinitas (the yellowing). The final stage is called Rubedo (the reddening). This is where the Philosopher's Stone is formed, which is said to be red in color.

THE ESSENTIAL FIFTH

Besides the four elements, the alchemists believed in a fifth element, which is actually the Anima Mundi or Materia Prima interacting and vitalizing the other four. This is known as the Quinta Essentia, which is the origin of the word quintessence. This hidden substance is exposed when the Philosopher's Stone is created. The fifth element may also be thought of as Ether, the incorruptible substance that the planets and stars were thought to be made of. Because they are so illusive the Quinta Essentia and the Philosopher's Stone are usually depicted as a mystical diagram called a mandala.

Figure 5.3 *The Philosopher's Stone and the Quinta Essentia depicted as a mandala.* (Robert M. Place)

THE SEVEN-RUNG LADDER

Like the ancient Babylonians, the alchemists equated the

(continues on page 96)

An Alchemical Mandala

Figure 5.4 is an alchemical symbolic diagram, or mandala, from the *Museum Hermeticum*, 1625, that contains references to much of the symbolism discussed in this chapter. In the center is the face of the alchemist, framed in a triangle, with the symbols of the three essences placed at the corners: clockwise from one o'clock, mercury, salt, and sulphur. The larger triangle, outside the circle, depicts their relationship to mind, body, and soul, and to the moon, the earth, and the sun. Within the circle, there is a seven-pointed star with the alchemical symbols of the seven metals, which are the same as the astrological symbols for the corresponding planets, assigned to the points: starting at one on the bottom, Saturn/lead, Jupiter/tin, Mars/iron, Sol/gold, Venus/copper, Mercury/quicksilver, and Luna/silver. Between the points are circles containing images that symbolize seven alchemical operations, from death or putrefaction on the bottom left to rebirth or resurrection on the bottom right.

Notice that the alchemist has one foot on the sea and one on land representing the wet and the dry but also the elements water and earth. The element air is symbolized by the feather in his left hand and fire by the candle in his right. Above his head are wings representing Ether, or the fifth element. In the lower corners is the Red King, with the sun on his head, sitting on a lion representing earth, and the White Queen, with the moon on her head, sitting on a whale representing water. In the upper corner on the left is a salamander, a mythic animal that lived in fire, and on the right an eagle for air. Because they are assigned to the corners in this way, they form a mystical pattern called a quincunx. The alchemist is in the quintessential or sacred position in the center of this design.

The inscription around the outer edge of the circle reads, *Visita Interiora Terrae Rectifando Inveniesn Occultum Lapidem* (visit the interior of the earth and in purifying you discover the hidden stone). The initials of this

Figure 5.4 *The alchemist's face appears at the center of this alchemical mandala.* (*Museum Hermeticum* [1625])

sentence spell Vitriol, which is the Secret Fire, the driving force of the transformation. Below the lion there is a fire-breathing dragon in a cave, a symbol of the Secret Fire, which is a hidden form of the Quinta Essentia. Because the dragon is hidden in the earth, he is also the answer to the puzzle posed by the inscription on the circle.

TABLE 5.4: **Correlations for the Seven Planets**

PLANET	METAL	OPERATION
Sun	Gold	Tincture
Moon	Silver	Coagulation
Mercury	Quicksilver	Distillation
Venus	Copper	Putrefaction
Jupiter	Tin	Calcination
Mars	Iron	Sublimation
Saturn	Lead	Solution

(continued from page 93)

seven ancient planets to seven metals (see Table 5.4), which they believed could be transformed, one to another, from the most base, lead, to the best, gold. Essentially they believed that all metals were made of the same substance and that their distinct characters were caused by impurities. Lead was the most corrupted and gold was the best because it was pure. This transformation, therefore, represented an ascent to a higher, purer state as the metals progressed to gold.

The alchemists also thought of the chemical processes in the Opus as a ladder leading them to gnosis. They would compose lists of seven principle processes. These lists, however, would differ from one text to another, and were arrived at by combining several processes under the name of another until the list is reduced to seven. The list in Table 5.4 is only one possible example.

THE TWELVE

Because the Magnum Opus was referred to as the year and thought to go through the 12 signs of the zodiac, alchemists sometimes made lists of 12 principle chemical operations that comprised the Magnum Opus instead of seven. The 12 signs of the zodiac were also equated to 12 chief substances.

6

The Synthesis of Magic, Alchemy, and Kabalah

It was a Tuesday night in 1873 at the New York lodge of the Brotherhood of Freemasons. Duncan was to be initiated into the first degree of the brotherhood on this night, and the room had been prepared for the ritual. In the center of the room there was a square wooden altar flanked on three sides by large bronze candlesticks with white candles burning steadily in the still room. On the altar was a large open Bible. Placed on top was a workman's compass and square, interlocked to form a diamond shape.

Behind the altar stood the Master Mason, who would preside over the ritual. Although he was dressed in a formal suit and top hat, he also wore a workman's leather apron with mystical symbols embroidered on the front. In his right hand he held a gavel, the symbol of his authority. Placed around the room in strategic locations were six other members of the lodge. Duncan was kneeling before the altar, but for now he was unaware of these arrangements because he was blindfolded. As he waited a drop of sweat rolled down his temple. As part of the ritual, Duncan was about to be symbolically murdered and resurrected.

SECRET SOCIETIES

It was the development of modern science in the seventeenth and eighteenth centuries that demoted alchemy from a science and mystical philosophy to a superstition in Western thinking. Similarly, magic was demoted during this same period. This is not surprising because modern science was founded on the ideas that the world functions like a machine composed of nonliving matter, that there is a separation between mind and matter that cannot be bridged, and that the contents of dreams and imagination are not a valuable area of study. These ideas are the complete opposite of the basic premises of the Hermetic philosophy that are the cornerstones of occult thought.

During this period, however, occultism did not die out. Instead, a great synthesis occurred in which magic, alchemy, Hermeticism, and Kabalah were united into one occult system. This synthesis often attempted to include science in the mix as well. At this time occultists tended to gather in secretive societies where members could rise in rank as they learned more about their system.

ROSICRUCIANS

One of the first examples of both of these trends was the Rosicrucian Brotherhood in Germany. Founded in the early 1600s, the Rosicrucians sought nothing less than the synthesis of all human knowledge, both scientific and occult, into one philosophy that could be taught to its members. This knowledge would prepare the world for the coming age of enlightenment, or new age, when the occult truths would be known by most people.

The Rosicrucians owe their start to three pamphlets written by an unknown author or authors published successively in 1614, 1615, and 1617, in Germany, called *Fama Fraternitatis Rosae Crucis* (The Famous Brotherhood of the Rosy Cross), *Confessio Fraternitatis Rosae Crucis* (The Confessions of the Brotherhood of the Rosy Cross), and *The Chemical Wedding of Christian Rosenkreutz*. These books talked about a secret mystical society founded around 1407 by the mythical Christian Rosenkreutz, an alchemist who traveled to Egypt, Palestine, and Fez, Morocco, studying the ancient mysteries and who achieved enlightenment. In *The Chemical Wedding* Rosenkreutz was

Figure 6.1   *An early form of the Rosicrucian emblem depicts a cross centered on a heart, which is centered on a rose. Compare this emblem to the image of the Philosopher's Stone in Figure 5.3, which features a cross, a heart, and a rosebud.* (Robert M. Place)

said to have magically created an artificial bride and groom who were married, killed, and resurrected in an operation reminiscent of the alchemical Great Work.

According to the first pamphlet, Rosenkreutz's wisdom was said to stem from a tradition that stretched back to ancient Egypt. Because he was dissatisfied with the institutions in his lifetime, Rosenkreutz founded his own brotherhood in Germany to pass on this tradition.

He meant to have his brothers offer cures to the sick without charge. When he died at the age of 106, Rosenkreutz was buried in a tomb by the brothers with instructions to keep the brotherhood secret until the tomb was reopened. The pamphlet claimed that Rosenkreutz's tomb was rediscovered and opened in 1604. The tomb was described as a seven-sided room illuminated by an artificial sun on the ceiling, as if by an electric light. The walls were covered with magical symbols connecting them with the seven planets, and in the center was a stone altar. What was most miraculous, however, was that when the altar was opened, the body of Christian Rosenkreutz was discovered inside totally preserved without decay, like a saint, and clutching a book of his sacred teachings.

Although the society described in the pamphlets was imaginary, some people believed it may have been real and others might have wished it were. In response to this growing enthusiasm, a Rosicrucian society was founded. Generally, the Rosicrucians practiced alchemy but of a spiritual nature without working in a laboratory. They were, however, open to scientific endeavors that they believed should be combined with their spiritual goal. In many ways they offered a middle ground between science and religion, and it is believed that they influenced such notable scientists as Sir Isaac Newton (1643–1727), who developed the theory of gravity but was also an alchemist, and Johannes Kepler (1571–1630), who discovered the elliptical orbits of the planets but was also an astrologer. It is also believed that the Royal Society of London, founded in 1660, one of the first scientific organizations in the world, was modeled on a Rosicrucian idea called the Invisible College, intended to be a free sharing of knowledge among natural philosophers. It was at the Royal Society, however, that a formal separation was declared between science and religion.

In the seventeenth century Europe was also split between the Catholic and the Protestant religions and the two groups were often at war with each other. Although formed primarily of Protestants and frowned on by the Catholic Church, the Rosicrucians offered a middle ground in which spiritual aspirations were more important than religious affiliations. The Rosicrucians believed that their philosophy was one that embraced the mathematical mystical truths of sacred geometry that had been expressed in all ancient science and religion. They believed that these truths were evident in the construction of the masterpieces of ancient architecture, such as the great pyramids of Egypt and the Temple of Solomon. Newton, who is considered one of the greatest scientists of this period, also took time to investigate the spiritual significance of Solomon's Temple, carefully reconstructing the plan from biblical references. He felt that the temple was a sacred mandala, or magic square, that symbolized the spiritual world and spoke of the creation. In the eighteenth century Newton's observations bore fruit with his influence on a new fraternal society called the Freemasons.

FREEMASONS

Although there may have been Masonic lodges in Scotland as early as the seventeenth century, the first official Masonic Grand Lodge was founded in 1717, in London. By the 1730s lodges were founded in Ireland, Scotland, France, and even the American colonies. Like most secret societies, however, the Freemasons claim an origin for themselves in the distant past. According to legend, the first Freemason was Hiram, the architect and craftsman who built the Temple of Solomon in the tenth century B.C.E. In the process of building the temple Hiram learned the secret name of God, knowledge that gave him access to colossal magical power, which was usually available only to the high priest. When three workers demanded the name form Hiram, he refused to give up the secret and was killed for his effort.

Freemasons use the tools of stonemasons, not for physical work but to contemplate as symbols in their philosophical mystical practice, in the same way that Rosicrucians practice alchemy without the chemical experiments. In the Masonic ritual of initiation, a Mason acts out the death of Hiram and is reborn to the lodge. The twentieth century

Figure 6.2 *A ceremonial Masonic leather apron bears several symbols. Inside the circular ouroboros in the center is the primary Masonic symbol, the square and the compass joined, which is a reference to the alchemical squaring of the circle. The skull of Hiram is in the middle of that, and the landscape below is the Temple of Solomon with the two pillars, named Boaz and Jakin, in front. The great pyramids are in the bottom left corner.* (Manly P. Hall, *The Secret Teachings of All Ages* [1995])

occultist Manly P. Hall (1901–1990) compared this Masonic ritual to the ancient Egyptian mysteries based on the death and resurrection of Osiris. It is not surprising, therefore, that the Freemasons also claim the ancient Egyptians as a source of their knowledge.

Besides offering a mystical ritual and the ability to move up in grade as one learned and experienced more advanced programs, the

Freemasons were a charitable organization and had a strong influence on politics in the eighteenth and nineteenth centuries. Many people involved with the American and the French revolutions were Freemasons. In many ways the ideals of inalienable rights, freedom of speech, and separation of church and state that were advanced by these revolutions were the ideals that the Freemasons championed. Eight of the founding fathers who signed the Declaration of Independence were Freemasons, including Benjamin Franklin (1706–1790) and John Hancock (1737–1793). George Washington (1732–1799) was also a Freemason as was his ally, the Marquis de Lafayette (1757–1834), who fought with him in the Revolutionary War.

THE TAROT

Antoine Court de Gébelin (1724 or 1728–1784) was a highest degree Freemason in the Nef Soeurs Loge, a famous Parisian lodge that included the philosopher Voltaire (1694–1778) and the American inventor and statesman Benjamin Franklin as members. In 1772, de Gébelin sent out an invitation for subscriptions for his nine-volume encyclopedia of his occult observations titled *Monde Primitif* (Primitive World). His writing was so full of misconceptions and false ideas that the entire work would have been forgotten by now, if it were not for an observation that he made about the **Tarot** in volume eight, which came out in 1781 and took hold of the imagination of occultists.

The Tarot is a deck of cards that was first created in Italy in the early fifteenth century. It contains five suits. Four of the suits have 10 numbered cards, or pips, and four royal cards in each suit. This part of the deck is related to a modern playing card deck, like the kind used to play poker. But the fifth suit contains a parade of 22 cards containing mystical and worldly figures, such as the Fool, the Emperor, Justice, the Hermit, and the Wheel of Fortune. The Tarot is mostly known today as a deck used for divination or fortune-telling but originally, in the Renaissance, it was mostly used for playing games. The images in the fifth suit, however, are influenced

Figure 6.3 *The reverse of the Great Seal of the United States has a Masonic design meant to declare the spiritual aspirations of the nation. The Egyptian-style pyramid has 1776, the year of the founding of the United States, inscribed on its foundation in Roman numerals and the eye of God in the triangle as its capstone. The motto, translated from Latin, says, "He approves our beginning—a new order of the ages."*

by Renaissance Hermeticism and Neoplatonism as well as Christian symbols or icons.

The Tarot was not well known in Paris in Court de Gébelin's time. When he first discovered it he noticed that the Tarot contained visual references to Hermeticism, and he became very excited. He believed that in this humble card game he had found a collection of hiero-glyphs that had been passed on from an ancient Egyptian book of philosophy and magic. Perhaps it was the actual *Book of Thoth*. In fact, in his encyclopedia, de Gébelin suggests the name Tarot was derived from the Egyptian *ta-rosh*, which is said to mean the doctrine or science of Thoth, in other words *The Book of Thoth*. This is based on wishful thinking instead of facts. *Ta* and *rosh* are not ancient Egyptian words, and the French name Tarot is actu-ally derived from the older Italian name for the deck, *Tarocchi*, which is also not connected to Egypt.

Figure 6.4 *Antoine Court de Gebelin believed that the Tarot was actually a book of wisdom passed on through the generations from the first Egyptian magicians and priests.* (F. Huot, 1784)

In de Gébelin's "rectified" ver-sion of the Tarot, he equated the images in the Tarot's fifth suit with figures from ancient Egypt and the myth of Osiris. For example he renamed the Chariot, which depicted a crowned warrior standing in a chariot, "Osiris Triumphant," and he renamed the Devil as "Typhon," a Greek name for Osiris' enemy, Set. De Gébelin claimed that the Tarot was really a book of wisdom from the ancient masters, who were the first magicians and priests. To preserve this valuable text, the wise Egyptian priests disguised it as a pack of playing cards. They real-ized that disguised as a trivial game this book would evade those who would intentionally destroy it, and it would be faithfully copied for the purpose of amusement. In this form it was brought to ancient Rome and, in the fourteenth century, to France. Over the centuries, it had continued to exist unrecognized and ignored by scholars as something not worthy of study until de Gébelin in a flash of insight recognized its true worth. With this story de Gébelin was retelling in a new form one of the alchemical myths. In the myth the substance needed to start making the Philosopher's Stone, which is the most valuable thing in the world, is something common and overlooked by people every day.

After Court de Gébelin made his claims, the Tarot became a regular part of the occult synthesis. The French occultist and alchemist Etteilla (1738–1791) helped to popularize its use for divination. For

The Beast

Besides Waite and Smith the occultist most often associated with the influential occult society, the Golden Dawn, is the notorious magician, author, and mountain climber, Aleister Crowley (1875–1947), pronounced "CROW-lee" and rhymes with holy, as he would say. Crowley referred to himself as the Beast of the Apocalypse, a title that he claimed his mother, a religious fundamentalist, bestowed on him in his youth. Because he liked to dabble in sex magic and blood sacrifice, the newspapers referred to him as the "Wickedest Man in the World."[1] In spite of his egotism and sensationalism, some considered him a gifted magician and artist.

Crowley first became involved with the Golden Dawn in 1898 and soon managed to earn the hatred of Yeats, Waite, and MacGregor Mathers. In 1900 he helped to add to the turmoil that caused the break up of the society. While in Egypt in 1904, he founded his own occult movement called **Thelema**. Crowley said that the Egyptian god Horus contacted him and appointed him as the god's chosen prophet and scribe. Through his minister, Aiwass, Horus dictated a text to Crowley. The result was Crowley's most famous book, *The Book of the Law*, in which he laid out the official doctrine of the new Aeon of Horus. The most important rule of the doctrine, and the one most often quoted is, "Do what thou wilt shall be the whole of the Law."[2]

most occultists, however, the true value of the Tarot was as an ancient book written in hieroglyphs that contained the mysteries of magic and told how to reach enlightenment. Although the Tarot could be used as a personal oracle or the cards could be used as images in ritual magic, many occultists preferred to meditate on the images and use them like a philosophical alchemical text. In the following century this use was popularized by the French occultist and magician Eliphas Levi.

Figure 6.5 *Aleister Crowley founded the occult movement known as Thelema in 1904. The order's symbol can be compared to the Masonic symbol in Figure 6.2.* (Robert M.Place)

HIGH MAGIC

In the mid-nineteenth century, thanks to its rejection by science, interest in the occult was dying out. In spite of this, one man stepped forward and declared himself a magician. This man was Alphonse-Louis Constant (1810–1875), who preferred to call himself by the Hebraic equivalent of his name, Eliphas Levi. Levi, who was born in Paris, was a deacon in the Catholic Church, a talented artist, and a political activist who had spent time in jail for his views. In 1853 Levi's wife left him and the following year their daughter died. These personal tragedies seem to be the catalyst that caused him to embrace the occult. It was in this same year that he changed his name and wrote his first books on magic as Eliphas Levi. *The Doctrine of High Magic* came out in 1854, and the following year Levi completed a second volume titled *The Ritual of High Magic*.

Levi called his system **High Magic**. He considered it a mystical path to enlightenment. To him magic was a science designed to give people superhuman power, but this power was not to be used for vulgar tricks. Its true purpose was to transform oneself through self-mastery. Levi's magical system became the most complete syntheses of magical doctrines ever conceived. The key ingredients in Levi's synthesis were Kabalah, Hermeticism, alchemy, Pythagorean number symbolism, astrology, ceremonial magic based on the Renaissance grimoires, and most importantly the all-encompassing Tarot. He never wrote a book on any of one of these subjects alone, but his works cover all of these as one interconnected subject.

Levi, like de Gébelin, considered the Tarot to be *The Book of Thoth* but he believed that the Tarot was also based on the Hebrew Kabalah, an idea only hinted at by de Gébelin. For the minor suits, Levi made a correlation between the four letters of the Tetragrammaton and the four suits. The central component of Levi's synthesis, however, was his correlation between the 22 cards in the fifth suit, which he called keys, and the 22 letters of the Hebrew alphabet. In the Kabalah, all of the Hebrew letters are correlated with parts of human anatomy;

to celestial symbols, such as planets or signs of the zodiac; and to the paths on the Tree of Life. In Levi's system the Tarot keys, although they were not created with these symbols in mind, are joined to all of these correlations as well. Each of his books has 22 chapters. Each chapter relates in theme to the Tarot key of the same number, as if Levi was translating the hieroglyphical Tarot into French.

Levi's synthesis was also unified by his theory that all magic is accomplished by the manipulation of a universal magical energy, which he called the Astral Light. His theory of the Astral Light was influenced by the German physician Franz Anton Mesmer (1734–1815). Mesmer attempted to find scientific validation for the existence of psychic energy and coined the term *animal magnetism* to describe it. Although Mesmer's work led to the discovery and acceptance of hypnosis, his theory of animal magnetism could not be proven scientifically. All religions and mystical traditions, however, recognize the existence of a subtle psychic energy. In Christian mysticism it is called *grace*, the alchemists called it the *secret fire*, in India it is called *prana*, and in Japan it is called *chi*. It has various names in other cultures, but in modern culture it may be best known by the term coined in the film *Star Wars*: "the force."

Levi influenced most of the notable occultists of his century, including his student Paul Christian (1811–1877), who wrote *The History of Magic*, published in 1870. He also influenced the Swiss occultist and hypnotist, Oswald Wirth (1860–1943), who in 1889 published a redesigned occult Tarot of his own. Levi's work also had an impact on the French Rosicrucian Papus (1865–1916), who wrote 260 books on the occult, including *The Tarot of the Bohemians*, published in 1889. Perhaps Levi's most important influence, though, was in England.

In 1854, before he wrote his first book on High Magic, Levi visited London to meet with fellow occultists and conduct a necromantic ritual that he wrote about in his book. By the later half of the nineteenth century, interest in the occult had continued to grow in England. Unlike Levi, who initiated himself and professed his ideas openly, the English occultists preferred to meet in secret societies. The most

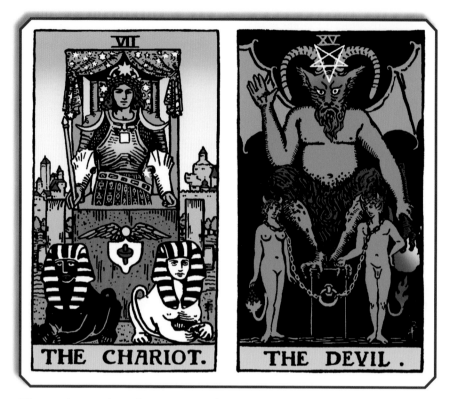

Figure 6.6 *Arthur Edward Waite and Pamela Colman Smith, creators of the Waite-Smith Tarot, were members of the Hermetic Order of the Golden Dawn, possibly the most powerful occult society in history. The Chariot and The Devil are two cards from the Waite-Smith Tarot.* (Arthur Edward Waite, The Pictorial Key to the Tarot (1910))

influential occult society in England was the Hermetic Order of the Golden Dawn. The Golden Dawn was founded in 1888 by the Rosicrucian and Mason Dr. William Wynn Westcott (1848–1925) and the Master Mason Samuel Liddell MacGregor Mathers (1854–1918).

The Golden Dawn was founded on a claimed connection with a German Rosicrucian order of the same name. There is no evidence of the older order, however, and it is believed that Westcott made it up. Although it was based on the Rosicrucian model, the Golden Dawn invited members of both sexes rather than including only males. It maintained a hierarchy of 10 grades, equated with the 10 sephiroth on the kabalistic Tree of Life. It taught a synthesis of occult topics, which included Hermeticism, Christian mysticism, Kabalah, alchemy, Egyptian mysteries, magic ritual, and, like Levi, Tarot. Some members tended to specialize in one or more of these subjects at the exclusion of the others, and after a little over 10 years, the initial order split into fragments. At its height, however, it had about 80 members, and it is possibly the most influential occult society of all time. Among the members of the Golden Dawn and the splinter groups were some of the best known occult figures of the day, such as the Irish poet William Butler Yeats (1865–1939), the actress Florence Farr (1860–1917), the notorious magician Aleister Crowley (1874–1947), the occult authors Dion Fortune (1890–1946) and Israel Regardie (1907–1985), and the creators of the most influential modern occult Tarot deck Arthur Edward Waite (1857–1942) and Pamela Colman Smith (1878–1951). The Golden Dawn's sphere of influence includes such notable people as the author of the Sherlock Holmes series, Sir Arthur Conan Doyle (1859–1930), and *Dracula* author, Bram Stoker (1847–1912).

Magic and Alchemy Today

Since the popularization of the New Age movement in the 1960s, many people in Western culture have been looking for a personal spiritual path that is not narrowed by the rules and restrictions of organized religions. As a result there has been renewed interest and investigation of traditional magic and alchemy. Today there are more opportunities to study the occult than at any time in recent history.

Freemasonry is still thriving throughout the United States. Although most lodges function primarily as social clubs, Scottish Rite Freemasonry is available for those interested in a mystical approach. The Rosicrucians have had a presence in the United States since colonial times. A new, more enterprising branch, called The Ancient and Mystical Order Rosae Crucis, abbreviated as AMORC, was founded by Harvey Spencer Lewis (1883–1939) in New York between 1909 and 1914. Today the AMORC is headquartered in San Jose, California, where they have built a complex of Egyptian-style buildings, including an Egyptian museum and a planetarium.

Although the Golden Dawn splintered in 1900 and the main branch died out in 1908, a new society, called The Hermetic Order of the Golden Dawn was founded by Chic Cicero in Columbus, Georgia, in 1977. It is not directly connected to the original society, but Cicero's Golden Dawn was founded with the help of Israel Regardie, who was a member of Stella Matutina, the Golden Dawn splinter group in London that refused to join with Waite's group. Regardie is the principle source for knowledge of the Golden Dawn rituals in the world today. The headquarters of Cicero's group is now in Elfers, Florida.

The German Masonic order called Ordo Templi Orientis (Order of the Temple of the East, abbreviated as O.T.O.) was founded between 1895 and 1906. In the early twentieth century Aleister Crowley transformed it into an institution for the teaching and preserving of his Thelemic philosophy. Today there are 45 branches of the O.T.O. in the United States. During the last year of his life, Crowley also spread his influence to the modern religion of **Wicca** when he met the English anthropologist Gerald B. Gardner (1884–1964), made him an initiate of the O.T.O., and instructed him in ceremonial magic.[1]

Figure 7.1 *A newer version of the Hermetic Order of the Golden Dawn, founded in 1977 under the same name, uses the symbol seen above.* (Robert M. Place)

A few years before, in 1939, Gardner claimed to have met a traditional coven of witches and been initiated into traditional English witchcraft. At this time he also joined "The First Rosicrucian Theater in England" founded by the Fellowship of Crotona, in New Forest. Some historians suspect that the coven was an invention of the Rosicrucian order. Gardner wrote about his experiences in two books, *Witchcraft Today*, 1954, and *The Meaning of Witchcraft*, 1959. He defined Witchcraft as an ancient religion and became the most influential advocate for what was either a revival of this religion or a totally new pagan religion. The new or revived religion, called Gardnerian Wicca, quickly spread through the British Isles and the United States, where along with it offshoots it survives today.

Besides participating in Wiccan rituals, one can also study shamanism in modern America, thanks to the anthropologist Michael Harner (born 1929). Harner wrote, *The Way of the Shaman*, published in 1980, and began conducting workshops to teach neoshamanism. In 1985 Harner founded The Foundation of Shamanic Studies, which publishes a magazine devoted to shamanism, called *The Shaman's Drum*.

Books about these organizations and people along with reprints of grimoires, such as *The Sacred Magic of Abra-Melin the Sage*; alchemical texts, such as *The Hermetic Museum* and the *Mutus Liber*; and kabalistic texts, such as *Sepher La-Bahir* and *Sepher ha-Zohar*, are available in most New Age or metaphysical book stores. Nowadays pop singers, like Madonna (born 1958), have made studying the Kabalah fashionable, and top-selling novels, such as the Harry Potter series and *The Da Vinci Code*, draw on magical and occult themes. Magic seems to be everywhere. Perhaps the most magical discoveries, however, have been made by scientists.

Scientists in the eighteenth century believed that an atom was the smallest indestructible particle of matter and that each element was composed of a different atom. This view began to unravel, however, in 1897, when electrons were identified as small, negatively charged pieces of the atom. Then in 1911, the English scientist Ernest Rutherford (1871–1937), discovered the atom's nucleus was composed of positively charged protons and neutrons

Figure 7.2 *Ernest Rutherford, New Zealand-born physicist, successfully transmuted nitrogen into oxygen by changing the number of its protons.* (World History/Topham/The Image Works)

with no charge. Rutherford found that the number of protons in the nucleus of a stable atom was always equal to the number of electrons in the shell, and that the number of protons in an atom determined which of the 118 elements it was. In 1919, Rutherford completed the alchemical dream when he transmuted the element nitrogen into oxygen by changing the number of its protons through the use of high-energy radioactivity. In 1941, two other physicists bombarded mercury with neutrons and transformed it into gold, proving that transmutation of a base metal into gold is possible.

The unraveling of eighteenth century science did not stop there. Since the 1950s quantum physicists have discovered more than 200 smaller particles within the atom. Rather than again redefining the term element, they chose to call them elementary particles. The most well-known elementary particles are the six quarks found inside the nucleus: up, down, top, bottom, strange, and charm. Science proved that the atom, once believed to be solid, is mostly space with some smaller particles moving inside. Now they wanted to know the nature of those smaller particles and the nature of matter itself.

In 1931 Wolfgang Pauli (1900–1958), the Austrian physicist famous for his work in quantum physics, worked with Carl G. Jung and helped him develop the theory of synchronicity discussed in the introduction.[2] This collaboration between Jung and Pauli illustrates that physicists had begun to question the

Figure 7.3 *Austrian physicist Wolfgang Pauli helped Carl G. Jung develop the theory of synchronicity, signaling the willingness of scientists to reinvestigate the occult.* (Mary Evans Picture Library/The Image Works)

materialistic assumptions of science. Quantum physics has demonstrated that elementary particles behave in ways that seem to defy common sense. They allow certain events to happen without a cause, unhinging the mechanical cause and effect view of reality; they defy assumptions about time and space because they can have either a location or a momentum but not both and separated particles act as if they are still joined; they also can be proven to be either a wave or a particle but the experiment designed to prove either will influence the results. At least at the subatomic level, science has demonstrated that the experimenter and the experiment cannot be separated. Therefore, there is a connection between mind and matter. Quantum physics has moved closer to the Hermetic view of reality. The examples of Pauli, who was a supporter of Jung's work, and Jung, who revived interest in both alchemy and Gnosticism as the precursors of psychology, show that some scientists are ready to reinvestigate the occult.

Timeline

Circa 40,000 B.C.E.   Homo sapiens migrate to Europe, where they create cave art and other art objects that seem to relate to shamanic magical practices.

Circa 10,000   Humans enter the Neolithic Period, or New Stone Age, begin to farm, and live in villages; shamans adapt to the needs of farmers and new religions develop with priests who practice ceremonial magic.

Circa 3500   The Sumerians become the first people to develop writing and, therefore, written history, and build the first ziggurats.

Circa 3150   The Egyptians settle in the Nile Valley and develop a complex religion centered on magical rites designed to assure the immortality of the soul.

Circa 2560   The Great Pyramid of Giza is completed in Egypt.

2350   The Akkadians conquer the Sumerians, and develop astrology.

2000–1825   The patriarch of the Hebrew people, Abraham, leaves the Babylonian city of Ur and brings his people to what is now Israel, where he founds the Jewish religion.

1792–1750   The Babylonian ruler Hammurabi unifies Mesopotamia under Babylonian rule and culture.

1323   The boy pharaoh Tutankhamun is entombed.

Circa 1000   One of the greatest magicians of all time, King Solomon, rules Israel and according to legend summons demons to do his bidding and build the Temple of Jerusalem.

Circa 600 The Persians conquer Mesopotamia and bring it into the larger Achaemenid Empire, which came to include Egypt; The Persian religion, Zoroastrianism, develops a complex system of angelology and demonology.

Circa 580–490 The great Greek philosopher, mathematician, and magician, Pythagoras, studies the wisdom of Mesopotamia and Egypt and founds a mystical sect in the Greek colony in Croton, Italy, in which numbers are seen as emanations.

490–430 The life of the Greek philosopher Empedocles, who developed the theory of the four elements.

Circa 428–347 The life of Plato, the great philosopher and mystic, who contributes the four qualities to the alchemical theory of the elements, provides the first description of the ladder of the seven planets, and provides a theory of the threefold structure of the soul.

332 Alexander the Great founds the city of Alexandria, Egypt, the greatest city of knowledge and learning in the ancient world.

100–300 C.E. The *Hermetica*, a collection of texts that teach alchemy and the magical philosophy that influences all Western occultism, is written in Alexandria.

100–700 Some time in this period the *Sepher Yetzirah*, which presents the mystical philosophy that became the basis for the Kabalah, is written in Palestine.

Circa 250 Zosimos, who lived in Panopolis, Egypt, is the first known historic alchemist.

313 The emperor Constantine paves the way for Christianity to become the official religion of the Roman Empire; black magic is outlawed but white magic is tolerated.

642 Arab culture discovers alchemy in Egypt.

Circa 721–815 The life of Arabian alchemist Jabir ibn Hayyan.

865–925 The life of Persian alchemist Mohammed ibn Zakariya al-Razi.

Circa 950 The Arabic alchemist Mohammed ibn Umail was active.

1100–1200 The Kabalah, a mystical or magical Jewish tradition, develops in Spain and southern France.

1144   Robert of Chester is one of the first to translate an Arabic alchemical text into Latin and, therefore, alchemy comes to Western Europe.

1236–1315   Influenced by the Kabalah and Sufism, the Spanish mystic Ramon Llull creates the Ars Magna.

1313–1418   The life of the famous alchemist Nicholas Flamel, who worked with *The Book of Abraham the Jew* to find the Philosopher's Stone.

1422   An ancient Greek book about Egyptian hieroglyphs, the *Hieroglyphica*, arrives in Florence, is translated into Latin, and initiates an interest in enigmatic symbolic art.

Circa 1450   The witchcraft executions begin in Europe.

1460   The *Hermetica* is brought to Florence and translated into Latin; it becomes a major influence on Renaissance thinking and magical tradition.

1463–1494   The Renaissance Neoplatonist, Pico della Mirandola, creates the Christian Kabalah.

1486–1535   The life of the famous occultist Heinrich Cornelius Agrippa, the author of *Occult Philosophy*.

1493–1541   The life of Paracelsus, one of the greatest alchemists and the founder of modern medicine.

1527–1609   The life of the famous English astronomer, mathematician, and magician John Dee.

1568–1622   The life of famous German alchemist Michael Maier.

1575–1624   The life of famous German alchemist Jacob Böhme.

1614, 1615, and 1617   The three pamphlets are published in Germany that started the Rosicrucian Brotherhood.

1717   The first official Masonic Grand Lodge is founded in London.

1743–1794   The life of the chemist Antoine Lavoisier, who redefined the term element and lowered alchemy to a pseudoscience.

1781   Antoine Court de Gébelin publishes the first article on the occult Tarot in volume eight of *Monde Primitif.*

1854 and 1855   Eliphas Levi publishes *The Doctrine of High Magic* and *The Ritual of High Magic*, and initiates a magical synthesis that includes, Kabalah, Hermeticism, magic, and Tarot

1870   Paul Christian's *The History of Magic* is published.

1888   The Golden Dawn is founded by Dr. William Wynn Westcott and Samuel Liddell MacGregor Mathers.

1889   Papus' *The Tarot of the Bohemians* is published.

1904   Aleister Crowley channels Horus in Egypt and writes the *Book of the Law*.

1909   Arthur Edward Waite and Pamela Colman Smith create the most famous occult Tarot.

1909–1914   AMORC, the American branch of the Rosicrucians, is founded in New York by H.S. Lewis.

1920s   Psychologist Carl G. Jung observes shamans in Africa and America and begins to incorporate active imagination, a shamanic-like technique, into his practice.

1922   Archeologist Howard Carter discovers Tutankhamun's tomb.

1931   Physicist Wolfgang Pauli works with Jung on the theory of synchronicity.

1951   The scholar of religion Mircea Eliade publishes *Shamanism: Archaic Techniques of Ecstasy* and defines shamanism for other scholars and scientists.

1954   Gardner's *Witchcraft Today* in published, causing interest in Wicca as a religion.

1977   The American Hermetic Order of the Golden Dawn is founded in Georgia.

1980   Michael Harner publishes *The Way of the Shaman: A Guide to Power and Healing*, and begins to teach neoshamanism in the United States.

1997   *Harry Potter and the Philosopher's Stone*, by J.K. Rowling, is released in Britain.

2003   *The Da Vinci Code*, by Dan Brown, is published.

Endnotes

INTRODUCTION

1. *Merriam Webster's Collegiate Dictionary: 10th Edition* (Springfield, Mass.: Merriam Webster, Inc., 1993), 699.

CHAPTER 1

1. E.A. Wallis Budge, *Egyptian Magic* (New York: Dover Publications, 1971), 10.
2. Ibid., 14–15.
3. Dan Burton and David Grandy, *Magic, Mystery, and Science: The Occult in Western Civilization* (Bloomington, Ind.: Indiana University Press, 2004), 31–33.

CHAPTER 3

1. Burton and Grandy, 154.
2. Ibid., 151–158.
3. Kurt Seligmann, *The History of Magic and the Occult* (New York: Harmony Books, 1975), 13–14.

CHAPTER 5

1. Adam McLean, *The Rosary of the Philosophers: Magnum Opus Hermetic Sourceworks No. 6* (London: Hermetic Research Trust, 1980), 42.

CHAPTER 6

1. Rosemary Ellen Guiley, *Harper's Encyclopedia of Mystical & Paranormal Experience* (New York: HarperSanFrancisco,1991), 129.
2. Aleister Crowley, *Magick: In Theory and Practice* (New York: Castle Books, 1929), xxii.

CHAPTER 7

1. Guiley, 131.
2. Burton and Grandy, 25.

Glossary

ACTIVE IMAGINATION   A Jungian term for interacting with dream images while awake

ALCHEMY   An ancient magical technology focused on the transmutation of substances and on the spiritual transformation of the practitioner that is also the forerunner of modern medicine, chemistry, and physics

AMULETS   See TALISMANS

ARS MAGNA   A thirteenth century Christian kabalistic system developed by The Spanish mystic Ramon Llull (also spelled Lully)

ASTROLOGY   The study of the relationship between the planets and constellations and human behavior and destiny

CEREMONIAL MAGIC   Ritual magic that involves the use of costumes and props, a prepared setting, and often involves a written or memorized incantation

DEMON   In biblical tradition a term for a fallen angel, one who has revolted against God's authority, but it may be used to refer to an evil or destructive spirit from any tradition; the term, however, is derived from the Greek term *daemon*, which referred to a spirit that was not necessarily good or evil.

DIVINATION   The practice of contacting spirits or gods to learn things that you can not learn through ordinary investigation with the five senses, such as the likely outcome of a situation or where something is that is lost or hidden

EMANATION   The belief that the creation of the world took place in stages, or emanations, that flow out of one another or give birth to one another instead of happening all at once; mystics may use the emanations, visualized in reverse order, as steps to a higher state of consciousness

ETEMENANKI   The great step pyramid or ziggurat in Babylon that is believed to have had seven steps or layers symbolizing the seven ancient planets

GEMATRIA   A kabalistic practice based on the fact that letters in Hebrew have numerical value and that the letters in words can be added and compared to other words with the same sum

GENIES   A spirit found in Islamic cultures that is powerful but not necessarily good or evil

GNOSIS   An ancient Greek word, pronounced "no-sis," for enlightenment; seekers of gnosis may be called Gnostics but the term is mostly used to refer to Christian seekers

GRIMOIRES   Pronounced "grim-wars," rhymes with guitars; magical text books that began to appear in the late Middle Ages.

HERMETICA   A collection of magical and philosophical texts written in Alexandria in the first to third centuries that are attributed to the mythical author Hermes Trismegistus and lay the ground for Western magical beliefs

HIGH MAGIC   The magical synthesis developed by Eliphas Levi

KABALAH   A Jewish mystical and magical tradition

MAGIC   The technology of working with the imagination to effect physical and psychological reality; Aleister Crowley preferred to spell it magick.

MAGIC CIRCLE   A protective circle drawn on the floor or ground and used in summoning a spirit or demon

MAGIC SQUARES   A magical device in which letters of words are written in rows to fill a square and designed to be read from more than one direction

MANDALA   A work of art that forms a map of the sacred universe depicting the sacred center and the four directions: north, south, east, and west

NECROMANCY   The practice of magically summoning the dead, usually for the purpose of divination

NEOPLATONISM   A group of Western mystical philosophies that synthesize Plato with other mystical philosophies

PENTACLES OR PENTAGRAMS   Circular magical designs used in rituals to summon spirits, for protection, or used as talismans; the most common has a five-pointed star in the center.

PUFFERS   Alchemists who were only interested in changing lead into gold to get rich

SEPHIROTH   The ten energized centers or emanations the comprise the Kabalistic Tree of Life. The singular form is sephirot.

SHAMAN   The anthropological term for a person who has the ability and training to enter a trance state and communicate with spirits so that he or she can help people; the plural form is shamans; in the past they have been called magicians, witch doctors, medicine men, sorcerers, or witches.

SORCERER   A practitioner of black magic

SUFISM   The beliefs and practices of a sect of Islamic mystics

SYMPATHETIC MAGIC   Magic that is practiced on an image or work of art, such as a voodoo doll, that is intended to effect the being or object that the art represents

SYNCHRONICITY   A Jungian term for an event happening in the physical world that coincides with an event happening in the mind, together in time, in a way that the mind feels is magically meaningful

TALISMANS   Symbolic objects or works of art that are empowered through a magic ritual and causes magical effects; sometimes a talisman is distinguished from an amulet in that an amulet is for magical protection and a talisman is for magically attracting beneficial effects, but most often the two terms are used interchangeably

TAROT   A deck of 78 cards now commonly used in divination and for occult purposes; composed of five suits; four minor suits that are similar to regular playing cards and a fifth suit with 22 mystical figures

TETRACTYS   A Pythagorean symbol of emanation consisting of a triangular arraignment of 10 dots with one at the top, two on the second layer, three on the third, and four at the base

TETRAGRAMMATON   The four-letter name of God in Hebrew, usually transliterated as Yahweh or Jehovah and comprised of the letter: yod, heh, vau, and heh

THELEMA   The magical philosophy developed by Aleister Crowley

URHEKAU   A magic wand with a carved snake head tip used by an Egyptian priest

WICCA   A modern religion based on traditional witchcraft

WORDS OF POWER   The words that gave power to a magic spell; chief among them were the magical names of gods and spirits; when used to summon a spirit they may be called an incantation

Bibliography

Barry, Kieren. *The Greek Qabalah*. York Beach, Maine: Samuel Weiser, 1999.

Budge, E. A. Wallis. *Egyptian Magic*. Gloucester, U.K.: Dodo Press, 2008.

Burton, Dan, and Grandy, David. *Magic, Mystery, and Science: The Occult in Western Civilization*. Bloomington, Ind.: Indiana University Press, 2003.

Cotnoir, Brian. *The Wiser Concise Guide to Alchemy*. San Francisco: Wiser Book, 2006.

Crowley, Aleister. *Magick: In Theory and Practice*. New York: Castle Books, 1929.

de Givry, Emile Grillot. *Picture Museum of Sorcery, Magic, and Alchemy*. Whitefish, Mont.: Kessinger Publishing, 2003.

Eliade, Mircea. *The Forge and the Crucible: The Origins and Structures of Alchemy*. New York: HarperCollins, 2000.

Eliade, Mircea. *Shamanism: Archaic Techniques of Ecstasy; Bollingen Series*. Princeton, N.J.: The Princeton University Press, 2004.

Gilchrist, Cherry. *The Elements of Alchemy*. Longmead, Dorset, England: Element Books, 1991.

Guiley, Rosemary Ellen. *Harper's Encyclopedia of Mystical & Paranormal Experience*. New York: HarperSanFrancisco, 1991.

Guiley, Rosemary Ellen. *The Encyclopedia of Witches, Witchcraft and Wicca, 3d ed.* New York: Facts On File, 2008.

Halevi, Z'ev ben Shimon. *Kabbalah: Tradition of Hidden Knowledge*. London: Thames and Hudson, 1988.

Hall, Manly P. *The Secret Teachings of All Ages*. Los Angeles: The Philosophical Research Society, 1995.

Holmyard, E. J. *Alchemy*. New York: Dover Publications, 1990.

Jung, Carl G. *Alchemical Studies*. From The Collected Works of C. G. Jung, vol. 13. Princeton, N.J.: Princeton University Press, 1967.

Jung, Carl G. *Psychology and Alchemy*. 2d ed. From The Collected Works of C. G. Jung, vol. 12. Princeton, N.J.: Princeton University Press, 1953.

Jung, Carl G. *Psychology and the Occult*. New York: Routledge, 2008.

King, Francis. *Magic: The Western Tradition*. New York: Avon Books, 1975.

Kingsley, Peter. *Ancient Philosophy, Mystery, and Magic: Empedocles and Pythagorean Tradition*. Oxford: Clarendon Paperbacks, 1995.

Klossowski de Rola, Stanislas. *Alchemy: The Secret Art*. London: Thames and Hudson, 1973.

Klossowski de Rola, Stanislas. *The Golden Game: Alchemical Engravings of the Seventeenth Century*. London: Thames and Hudson, 1998.

Knight, Gareth. *Magic and the Western Mind*. St. Paul, Minn.: Llewellyn, 1995.

Levi, Eliphis. *Transcendental Magic: Its Doctrine and Ritual*. New York: Samuel Weiser, 1970.

McLean, Adam. *The Alchemical Mandala*, 2d ed. Grand Rapids, Mich.: Phanes Press, 2002.

McLean, Adam. *The Rosary of the Philosophers: Magnum Opus Hermetic Sourceworks No. 6*. London: Hermetic Research Trust, 1980.

Ogden, Daniel. *Magic, Witchcraft, and Ghosts in the Greek and Roman Worlds: A Sourcebook*. Oxford: Oxford University Press, 2009.

Pinch, Geraldine. *Magic in Ancient Egypt*. Austin: University of Texas Press, 1994.

Place, Robert M. *The Symbolism of Alchemy*. Saugerties, N.Y. and Portland, Ore.: Hermes Publications, 2008.

Place, Robert M. *The Tarot: History, Symbolism, and Divination*. New York: Tarcher/Penguin, 2005.

Rulandus, Martinus. Translated by A.E.Waite. *A Lexicon of Alchemy*. York Beach, Maine: Samuel Wiser, 1984.

Scott, Walter, editor and translator. *Hermetica: The Ancient Greek and Latin Writings Which Contain Religious or Philosophic Teachings Ascribed to Hermes Trismegistus Vol. I*. Boston: Shambhala Publications, 2001.

Seligmann, Kurt. *The History of Magic and the Occult*. New York: Harmony Books, 1975.

Stillman, John Maxson. *The Story of Alchemy and Early Chemistry*. Whitefish, Mont.: Kessinger Publishing, 2003.

Von Franz, Marie-Louise. *Alchemy*. Toronto: Inner City Books, 1981.

Von Franz, Marie-Louise. *Psyche and Matter*. Boston and London: Shambhala Publications, 2001.

Waite, Arthur Edward, translator. *The Hermetic Museum*. Metairie, La.: Cornerstone Book Publishers, 2007.

Further Resources

WEB SITES

The Alchemy Web site
http://www.alchemywebsite.com/index.html
An online alchemical resource with tens of thousands of pages of information.

Mystical Keys
http://mysticalkeys.com/library
This site is devoted to the study of the Hermetic Kabalah.

International Web Site for the Ancient and Mystical Order Rosae Crucis
http://www.amorc.org
This site is a worldwide directory of Rosicrucian groups.

Amsterdam Hermetica—Western Esotericism in the Academy
http://www.amsterdamhermetica.nl
This is the University of Amsterdam's site devoted to Western esotericism.

GoldenDawnPedia
http://www.goldendawnpedia.com
This site is an online encyclopedia of the Golden Dawn.

The Hermetic Order of the Golden Dawn Web Site
http://www.hermeticgoldendawn.org
This is the official web site of the American branch of the
Golden Dawn

Tarotpedia
http://www.tarotpedia.com/wiki/Main_Page
This is a site dedicated to the study of the Tarot.

Index

Page numbers in *italics* indicate illustrations.

About the Author

ROBERT M. PLACE is an author and a visionary artist and illustrator whose award-winning works in painting and sculpture have been displayed in galleries and museums in America, Europe, and Japan and have graced the covers and pages of numerous books and publications. He is the designer, illustrator, and co-author, with Rosemary Ellen Guiley, of *The Alchemical Tarot* and *The Angels Tarot*. He is the designer, illustrator, and author of *The Buddha Tarot*, *The Tarot of the Saints*, and *The Vampire Tarot*. He is the author of *The Buddha Tarot Companion* and *The Tarot: History, Symbolism, and Divination*, which Booklist has said, "may be the best book ever written on ... the tarot." For *Mysteries, Legends, and Unexplained Phenomena*, he has also authored *Astrology and Divination* and *Shamanism* and is the cover illustrator for the series. His Web site is http://thealchemicalegg.com.

About the Consulting Editor

ROSEMARY ELLEN GUILEY is one of the foremost authorities on the paranormal. Psychic experiences in childhood led to her lifelong study and research of paranormal mysteries. A journalist by training, she has worked full time in the paranormal since 1983, as an author, presenter, and investigator. She has written 41 nonfiction books on paranormal topics, translated into 14 languages, and hundreds of articles. She has experienced many of the phenomena she has researched. She has appeared on numerous television, documentary, and radio shows. She is a columnist for *TAPS Paramagazine* and a consulting editor for *FATE* magazine. Ms. Guiley's books include *The Encyclopedia of Angels*, *The Encyclopedia of Magic and Alchemy*, *The Encyclopedia of Saints*, *The Encyclopedia of Vampires, Werewolves, and Other Monsters*, and *The Encyclopedia of Witches and Witchcraft*, all from Facts On File. She lives in Maryland and her Web site is http://www.visionaryliving.com.